In *Take Me to the Water*, Starlette Th  he
prevailing perspectives on the sociop(;ee
others, and as a framework in which ice
permeates much of Christian religious of
race must be dismantled and removed trom tne lite and teachings ot the church. Thomas seeks
to reconstruct a gospel narrative that omits biases, hierarchies, and perspectives shaped by race.
In so doing, she is committed—in her own words—to "work toward an inward orientation that
not only changes our perspectives...but challenges the systems that support social othering."
—Jeffrey Haggray, Executive Director, American Baptist Home Mission Societies

With sound scholarship and great passion, Starlette Thomas offers an indictment of the North
American church's embrace of the false construct of race. More powerfully, she speaks with the
voice of a prophet urging us to remember who we are, pushing us to return to those heady,
beginning days of the early church when Christians were rising out of the water a new people,
one people. While calling out European colonialists and their descendants, *Take Me to the Water*
nevertheless invites all readers to wade in our baptismal waters and come to know our kinship
with each other through it. Thomas offers history, study guides, and an action plan to help us
take the plunge into a raceless community. Like the people of Nineveh, will we heed her call?
—Bren Dubay, Executive Director, Koinonia Farm, Americus, Ga.

Starlette Thomas provides the church with a gift, though be sure to open it slowly and don't expect
sugar-coated junk. In an age of shallow theology and scorching bigotry, Thomas challenges us to
enter the deeper waters. I'm a Baptist who believes in congregational freedom, so I won't suggest
making this required reading at churches, but Christians who long for a better gospel than the
one given us over the past 400 years should definitely read this book. —Brian Kaylor, President
and Editor-in-Chief, *Word & Way*

The bloody house of American racism is deconstructed board by board down to the studs
and nails in this remarkable book by Starlette Thomas. Don't be afraid of that dissertation-
like subtitle; it's a mouthful but her statement of purpose clearly interprets for us: "the raceless
gospel expressed through baptismal identity can act as a catalyst for desegregating sacred space."
Eloquently concise or as I would say, BOOM. As you read, you will be treated to a vibrant
intellect as she engages history, theology, sociopolitical, and cultural ramifications of identity
and a preacher who has, like a Gullah basket weaver, coiled and wrapped numerous strands into
her book/basket. Use it to sift the debris of a culture in love with death. Use it to carry the fruits
of liberation. The bibliography she provides is all by itself worth the price. You will be given a
decoding device that unlocks baptismal identity as a fierce counter-sign to the present age of
Christian nationalism and white supremacy. —R. Michael Bledsoe, Retired Church History
Professor, Howard University School of Divinity; Retired Pastor, Riverside Baptist Church,
Washington, D.C.

Take Me to The Water invites readers to reimagine how our new birth in God's family requires
us to see through the lenses of Christ and embrace each other as members of the one family.
Drawing from the experiences of the once-enslaved, Starlette Thomas walks us through the
pages of the slave narrative, painting a picture of a segregated church with its roots etched in the
sociopolitical construct of race. Using water baptism as a catalyst for a unifying church, this book
helps us "to deconstruct race and decolonize identity." *Take Me to the Water* should be required
reading for anyone serious about breaking down the walls of segregation and giving birth to a
unified church.—Emmett L. Dunn, Executive Secretary-Treasurer/CEO, Lott Carey Baptist
Foreign Mission Convention

With philosophical precision and provocative prose, Starlette Thomas shows us there is something about the water of baptism that has the power to divest us of the lie of race and desegregate Christian communities in America. As a profound theological reflection, compelling personal confession, and catalyzing small group curriculum, *Take Me to the Water* has the potential to raise the church to new life, liberated from the bonds of a racialized faith through the clarion call of a raceless gospel. Read and be reborn!—**Ben Boswell, Senior Minister, Myers Park Baptist Church, Charlotte, N.C.**

In this sharp interrogation of American Christianity's insistence on perpetually attempting to harness the power of the gospel to fuel our own race-framed interests, Thomas applies sharp scholarship, her trademark wit, and a tenacious conviction that the God we say we serve has no use for the designations we impose. Read this book. Use it to spur discussion. Read it to remember that God's spirit flows with a power we will never control.—**Amy Butler, Founder, Invested Faith**

This poetically written and theologically rigorous book takes the reader into the deep waters. It is well researched, challenging, and as one would expect from Thomas, in places controversial. For those committed to lifelong learning, this is the book to read. There are new gems in every paragraph.—**Wale Hudson-Roberts, Racial Justice Coordinator, Baptist Union**

In *Take Me to the Water,* Starlette Thomas challenges us in raw and powerful ways to take on the racial divide and racist past and present. Her scriptural, social, and theological observations are uniquely eloquent indeed. To put it even more strongly, this is a prophetic word of things we need to engage. Most importantly, this work is not only poignantly descriptive, but also in its working questions and suggested liturgy is practically prescriptive. Thomas' raceless gospel and its subsequent work in *Take Me to the Water* are places that we need to be, renewing both our baptismal commitments and vows to the glory of God and the renewal of ourselves and others whom we serve.—**Jeremy Bell, General Secretary, North American Baptist Fellowship**

Starlette Thomas leads us to and through the water. She tells us: "I don't simply have a problem with race but believe that race is the problem with our shared human being and belonging. I have no interest in working with the word, so don't add this book to your anti-racism reading list. I am anti-race." With these words she beckons us to join her on a journey toward understanding, liberation, and healing. For too long, too many Christians have used and continue to use their religious texts and platforms to teach ignorance and maintain unbelonging for some—whether Christian or not—and perpetual belonging for an increasingly short list of others. Thomas illustrates how productive fresh "raceless" understandings of the gospel uphold its message of wholeness for all humans and effectively undo the human-made divisions among us. For anyone who wants to truly practice what they preach, *Take Me to the Water* is a must read, with Dr. Thomas showing readers how to de-racialize Christianity.—**Sheena Mason, Assistant Professor, SUNY Oneonta; author of *The Raceless Antiracist: Why Ending Race Is the Future of Antiracism***

For those of us who have had the blessing of working with and hearing Rev. Thomas preach and teach, we have experienced a mode of love, a part of our own history, and the challenges that are before us.—**Lawrence Michael Cameron, Pastor, Bethany Union Church, Chicago**

"TAKE ME TO THE WATER"

The Raceless Gospel as Baptismal Pedagogy
for a Desegregated Church

STARLETTE THOMAS

© 2023
Published in the United States by Nurturing Faith Inc., Macon, GA,
www.goodfaithmedia.org

Library of Congress Cataloging-in-Publication Data is available.

ISBN: 978-1-63528-235-1

Unless otherwise indicated, scripture quotations are taken from the NRVS.

Dedication

To my ancestors who were forcibly converted by way of water during the European slave trade—from human beings to chattel property and whose names were washed away.

CONTENTS

Foreword

I was just seven years old when I was baptized. Many decades older now, I still remember that formative event more vividly than my service of ordination to Christian ministry in my mid-twenties or when I was commissioned an American Baptist home missionary years later.

Peering over the paper-thin balcony of time, I can see and hear the senior choir of the Tabernacle of Faith Baptist Church melodically encouraging me and other baptizands to step into the water. They sang, "Wade in the water. Wade in the water, children. God's going to trouble the water." I boldly entered the chilly baptismal pool on that warm first Sunday evening of August in 1958. First Sunday evenings at "the Tab" were exclusively reserved for baptisms and for participating in the Lord's Supper.

Even at that age, I had already witnessed dozens of these first Sunday services before I myself was finally allowed to be baptized and then invited to join in the commemorative meal afterward. I knew what I was doing. I knew Jesus. I had seen Jesus incarnated in the face of Brother Cathcart, the voice of Sister Reece, the prayers of Rev. Campbell, the generosity of Mr. and Mrs. Stokes. I saw Jesus through the hands, hearts, and lives of so many others, both in and out of my local church.

With his left hand on my shoulder, and his right supporting me from floating away, Pastor F. Douglass Ferrell looked me in my eyes and asked, "Son, do you commit all that you know about yourself to all that you know about Jesus, and will you do so for the rest of your life?"

Responding, "Yes, I do and yes I will," I was then immersed and initiated into a life-long journey and fellowship with others who had also promised to walk wet in the world, just as Jesus did when he emerged from the Jordan, a baptizand of John and the Holy Spirit.

As I write, I can still see and feel the cold water dripping from my white baptismal gown as I strode out of the pool into a new life and into the Beloved Community that greeted me. On that evening, I became one of the "As many of you as were baptized with Christ" that Paul proclaimed had entered into a counter-cultural narrative, believing and behaving as transformed non-conformists and citizens of a new world in his letter to the Galatians (3:27-28).

According to Paul, the efficacy of baptismal waters is more potent than human blood in human veins. Baptismal water does more than dilute and diminish sin. Baptismal waters empower us to grow to distain the privileged distinctions humans make with regards to Jew or Greek, slave or free, and male or female. When baptismal waters flow through the core of our being, barriers of exclusion are broken and bridges of embrace begin to replace them. This water makes us one in Christ Jesus.

In the pages that follow, Dr. Starlette Thomas applies this pedagogy to matters of "race" and its poisonous progeny in the North American church.

So very much of the church's theology, Christology, and ecclesiology have been impacted by this dehumanizing and ultimately *Imago Dei*-defacing social construct we all too often assume to be real. Thomas contends that baptismal water is capable of de-racializing a Christianity polluted by an anthropology that promulgates that only some people are real people, or that they are the only people who really count.

Starlette Thomas performs a valuable function herein by subjecting the Christian tradition to a critical analysis of the origins of race and its many death-dealing afterlives that have haunted the church and American society for centuries. With this text, she further demonstrates her craft as a ghostbuster. Pastorally and often poetically she deconstructs Western civilization's ineffable apparition called "race" that harasses human beings in the White House, our courthouses, and in houses of worship. In doing so, Thomas energizes people of faith to reclaim the prophetic mission of the church and so transform itself in its own life to become a witnessing community articulating the vision of the new humanity that the gospel proclaims.

Segregated churches are by default isolated and estranged churches. They quarantine themselves. There is no flow. There is no current. These churches may be described as having algae in their baptismal pool or font. *Take Me to the Water* is a pedagogical primer that helps us clean up our acts to make it safe for all of us to get back into the water again—or, perhaps for the first time.

Sisters and Brothers, with this book in hand, you have already demonstrated your desire to enter fresh waters. The material and exercises in this book will help take you there. As I reflect again on my own baptism all those decades ago, I remember the song the congregation sang as I emerged from the water, changed clothes, and prepared myself to join the waiting congregation sharing in communion together. It was this:

> On Jordan's stormy banks I stand,
> And cast a wishful eye
> To Canaan's fair and happy land,
> Where my possessions lie.
>
> I am bound for the promised land,
> I am bound for the promised land;
> O who will come and go with me?
> I am bound for the promised land.

Will you come and go with us? That "Kin-dom" awaits us. Let's step into the water.

Rev. Dr. Aidsand F. Wright-Riggins[*]

[*]Aidsand Wright-Riggins is executive director emeritus of the American Baptist Home Mission Societies, an affiliate faculty member of the Berkeley School of Theology, a board member of the Morehouse School of Religion, and the mayor of Collegeville, Penn.

Acknowledgments

From blog to book, the pages that follow represent more than a decade of writing this vision until I was clear of what I was seeing—not a post-racial society but a raceless "kin-dom" that is coming. These words came by day and by night, by invitation and in preparation for sermons, Bible studies, podcasts, lectures, workshops, and a post-graduate degree. These words came by way of a mixture of African American spirituality and Christianity, fashioned on a mourner's bench upon which I professed my faith and rose to proclaim an innate sense of "somebodiness." Like the ring shout, these words encircled and then came to me: "As many of you as were baptized with Christ have clothed yourselves with Christ. There is no longer Jew or Greek, there is no longer slave or free, there is no longer male and female; for all of you are one in Christ Jesus" (Gal. 3:27-28). These words then took hold of me.

I am certain that "somebody prayed for me." The ancestors, to include my grandparents, Eva Mae and John Curtis Thomas, prayed to be free of the ongoing experience of colonization, racialization, and white supremacy. They put their hands together and handed to me a southern ascetism coupled with a charismatic freedom of religious expression, which led to a mystical experience that was transcendent, ecstatic, and unitive. I, too, had prayed for relief from racialized oppression, and then these words delivered me—the raceless gospel.

But it took a lot of resisting, defying, and not shying away from what race really is and will always be: a social system of belief that divinizes, celebrates, and pedestalizes bodies socially-colored white and that would always demonize, scrutinize, and marginalize me. Consequently, I am indebted to Gabriel Prosser, Denmark Vesey, Nat Turner, and to all those unnamed freedom fighters who participated in rebellions, uprisings, and the undermining of American slavery. Thank you to the ancestors who refused to go along to get along with its progeny. Thank you for putting your body on the line so that I could read and write, think and speak, move and live freely.

I am also grateful to the many wordsmiths, word workers, and word conductors along the way who have guided my feet and transported me to a time that is meant to be, namely:

Harriet Tubman
W.E.B. Dubois
Ralph Ellison
James Weldon Johnson
Zora Neale Hurston
Howard Thurman
James Baldwin
bell hooks
Toni Morrison

I give thanks also for the work and witness of:

Carter G. Woodson
Marcus Garvey
Martin Luther King Jr.
El-Hajj Malik El-Shabazz
Alex Hailey
Frantz Fanon
Albert J. Raboteau
Cain Hope Felder
Frank M. Snowden
Derrick Bell
Mia Bay
Gayraud Wilmore
Peter Paris
James Cone
Kelly Brown Douglas
Dwight N. Hopkins
Gay Byron
Willie James Jennings
Brian Bantum
David R. Roediger
Nell Irvin Painter
M. Shawn Copeland
the late James H. Evans Jr.

I have come this far by the faith it took them to write about race in their own words and on their own terms.

Thank you to everyone who gathered in churches, colleges, community groups, denominations, and universities that have invited me to speak. I am especially grateful to the Servant Leadership School, now the School for Liberation in Washington, D.C., that gave me my first opportunity to share the raceless gospel as a one-day retreat. The Baptist World Alliance afforded me the space to present my first paper to the Commission on Racial and Gender Justice titled "Doing Justice to Our Bodies: How the Social Construct of Race Wrongs Us" in Zurich, Switzerland. The members of the Historic Bethany Union Church of Chicago and Pastor Larry Cameron trusted that the message was worthy of declaration during its 150th anniversary. Thank you to Steven Skultety, Adam Gussow, and Nathan Oakes. The students and community members who gathered at the University of Mississippi were receptive, and a few were even ready to believe in the possibility of this raceless "kin-dom." Thank you for an incredible discussion and the tear-filled fellowship that followed where we believed that it was possible to live race-free if for one night only.

Wesley Theological Seminary's Doctor of Ministry program, "Life Together," curated space and time that culminated in a treatise that energized me for the work ahead, some of which has been included. The faculty, staff, and members of my cohort offered feedback and suggestions that deepened my conviction and confession of what has become my calling. Our time together served as a testament that God was at work in me and through this message. All the right words came together, ushered in by the Spirit and my faculty reader, Dr. Josiah Ulysses Young III. Thank you, all.

I am especially grateful to Good Faith Media and its board members for its creation of The Raceless Gospel Initiative and calling me as its director. Thank you to the staff who support my ideas and encourage my creativity: Mitch Randall, John D. Pierce, Zach Dawes Jr., Cliff Vaughn, Tony W. Cartledge, and Missy Randall. This book wouldn't be in your hands if it were not for Tony W. Cartledge especially, who has shared my work with his students at Campbell University and is ensuring that it remains in circulation. Bruce Gourley, managing editor of publishing, treated my words like his own, and his brilliance remains a source of encouragement to keep writing as it can only get better. Jackie Riley, senior copyeditor, nurtured my words with helpful suggestions and ensured that the manuscript became a full-grown book. Cally Chisholm, creative coordinator for publishing and marketing, gathered my words together and ensured that they were print-ready. It took this village to raise this book and place it into your hands.

Thank you to Dr. Sheena Mason, who shares in this raceless journey and the conviction that there is another way to belong to ourselves and in community. Thank you to Rev. Dr. Aidsand Wright-Riggins who graciously contributed the foreword and is both a source of inspiration and encouragement. Thank you to my beautiful son, John Curtis, who is living proof that miracles do happen. And finally, to the water and to the depths it has taken me in my journey to becoming and belonging in this body, thank you.

Introduction

I tol' Jesus it would be all right
If He changed mah name
Jesus tol' me I would have to live humble
If He changed mah name
Jesus tol' me that the world would be 'gainst me
If He changed mah name
But I tol' Jesus it would be all right
If He changed mah name

I consider myself a race abolitionist, a dignity advocate, a community-building protagonist, a baptism evangelist. Through the work and witness of the raceless gospel, I am taking the North American church to the waters of baptism and submerging a Christian faith, identity, and practice that supports human hierarchies as well as the white supremacist ideology and theology that undergird them. With both hands on their cross and following in the footsteps of Jesus, I believe that Christians should have no interest in power-grabbing identities and ways of being.

I don't simply have a problem with race but believe that race is the problem with our shared human being and belonging. I have no interest in working with the word, so don't add this book to your anti-racism reading list. I am anti-race. Because there is no racial justice. Race was not created to be just. There is no racial equality. Race was not created with the belief that human beings are created equal. There is no racial unity. Race was created to divide us based on physical attributes such as shape of skull, size of nose, texture of hair, and pigment of skin. There is no racial reconciliation. Race was not created to bring us all together after helping us reconcile our differences.

When I say race, I'm talking about power and how we were swindled out of authority over our bodies—not identity or nationality. Because race has no country, no culture but colonialism. As a Christian, I don't believe that I am powerless against it. Instead, I believe in the water of baptism and its witness, its ability to draw out all our impurities and to drown out all the competing voices so that we can be our true selves.

The raceless gospel also encourages us to see race as it is—a sociopolitical construct, built from the tip of our tongues up, a human invention and what Brian Bantum describes as "a tragic incarnation." In the end, it is an invitation so beautifully explained by mystic and theologian Howard Thurman, who said, "I have always wanted to be *me* without making it difficult for you to be *you*."[1] This is my covenant, my promise to you as my next of kin.

This work will make a mess of things, starting with our boxes, categories, and containers for human identity, being, and belonging. It will require us to wade in the water and wade into the shared drama and trauma of American society. Don't worry: I'm here to walk alongside you, but it won't be easy.

Paul writes to the Romans, "Therefore we have been buried with him by baptism into death, so that, just as Christ was raised from the dead by the glory of the Father, so we too might walk in newness of life."[2] As baptized believers, this is not simply a new lease on life. We decrease and he increases in us.[3] We become an extension of Christ's body.

We don't merely identify *with* Christ, but we identify *as* Christ. C.S. Lewis believed that "every Christian is to be a little Christ." Submerged in womb water, we are born again, new creatures in Christ Jesus, new human beings. Titus calls baptism "the water of rebirth."[4] Jesus says that baptism of water and Spirit grants us entry. It takes water.

In John 3, Jesus tells Nicodemus about the birth "from above," but Nicodemus is only clear on the birds and the bees. He knows where babies come from. Jesus reiterates his point, and Eugene Peterson wrote it this way in *The Message*:

> Jesus said, "You're not listening. Let me say it again. Unless a person submits to this original creation—that 'wind-hovering-over-the-water' creation, the invisible moving the visible, a baptism into new life—it's not possible to enter God's kingdom."[5]

So then, we have got to come clean on a few things. Because Jesus says all it takes is water and the Spirit hovering, that new life in Christ doesn't mean a change in our weekly schedule but the ending of one life and the beginning of another. We are baptized and reborn as begotten children of God. We come up—headfirst, inhale first breath, and take first steps with Jesus.

Jesus' disciples are called to be "fishers of people"[6] but the church, now expressed through buildings though it began as a body, has become a fishbowl. Christians are just swimming around in the same old stagnant water because "we've always done it like this." Too afraid to filter it or to empty it, the North American church could use a fresh start—or better yet, a rebirth.

Many church leaders aren't making disciples. Instead, they are creating consumers of a religious product that is available in contemporary and traditional services, that comes with hymns or praise songs, that is offered at 8 a.m., 9 a.m., 10 a.m., or 11 a.m. There is also an evening service if that doesn't work for you. But Jesus doesn't work for us or around our schedules. We must have his church confused with a business, a 501 (c) 3 organization. We must have Jesus mixed up with a CEO or worse still, a salesman—though Jesus didn't leave his followers a business model.

Furthermore, it is also a religious product that they guilt persons into. "Look what Jesus did for you, a sinner. Get saved! Come to Jesus today!" Because "if you die tonight, do you know where you'd spend eternity?" People often come to Jesus out of fear and shame—not love and gratitude.

Some church leaders are selling a religious experience. We go to church to sit in a seat. But being a disciple of Jesus means we sit at his feet. Jesus said, "Learn of me"—not worship me.[7] Jesus never asked for the red-carpet treatment, for roped-off and VIP seating.

In fact, Jesus kept it moving. He told his disciples, "If any want to become my followers, let them deny themselves and take up their cross and follow me."[8] Start here: Clean up, get washed in this body of water, and then follow me. We have much to reflect on, and I think that baptism is a pool that offers this opportunity.

The state of the North American church is troubling with its belief in white supremacy, race, and its progeny; its practice of a half-baked patriarchy, half-priced misogyny, and half-hearted morality. With so much hypocrisy, it is no longer viewed as an expert or an authority. It has lost a generation or two's respect. Turned inward and focused on the needs of its members solely, those days are long gone, and the expectation of esteem is no longer a given.

The global pandemic caused by COVID-19 unsettled what many Christians believed about ourselves, our world, and the institutions that once gave our lives meaning. There is a moral reckoning occurring. Christians are looking at the words of Jesus and asking the church, "Have you practiced them lately?" These Christians are re-examining their beliefs and quietly leaving the church. They are at home faithfully deconstructing with the hope of piecing back together a healthier and more authentic ecclesiology. It's going to take time, and I think it takes us to the water.

John the Baptist is waving people over to the water. Camel hair is never going to be in style—even if you add a belt to it. But he was a prophet—not a fashion icon. The change that was coming would not be a topical or seasonal treatment.

To be sure, there were lots of people talking about God, using God in their sentences. But this was different. Really talking about God is hard, and it's rare—as confirmed in the Hebrew Scriptures when God called Samuel: "The word of the Lord was rare in those days."[9] Prophetic words that speak unapologetic truth to unhinged power, that challenge traditional hatreds and systemic oppression, that fight prejudice with unconditional love are rare.

People who put the words of Jesus into practice daily and who call us to live the life we sing about on Sunday morning are rare. Palatable words are cheap and easy to come by. It costs us nothing to say them, and these words don't add to the hearer at all. But talking about God changes us.

This is Thomas G. Long's conviction in *Testimony: Talking Ourselves Into Being Christian*. He writes that "saying things aloud is a part of how we come to believe. We talk our way toward belief, talk our way from tentative belief through doubt to firmer belief, talk our way toward believing more fully, more clearly, and more deeply."[10] Therefore, we must be careful with our words as we can just as easily talk ourselves out of something. Long says, "To speak about God is to live in that world and to speak out of it."[11] This talk is not cheap; this gospel speech is not proven by talking a good game.

The early Christians called it "the Way," as Jesus had a way of doing things that made him stand apart from all the would-be messiahs and prophets of his day. But a watered-down gospel shapes nothing. Our work and witness should "prepare the way of the Lord" without getting in the way of the Lord, without allowing persons to assume that you are the Lord. It should not encourage the belief that if you don't preach, then they can't hear the gospel; that if you aren't praying, then God won't answer them; that if you don't visit them, then they won't be healed.

The same was true for John the Baptist, who backed away and said in essence: "You've got the wrong person. I'm not the Messiah you are looking for. I may sound like him, but I am not him. I'm good but not that good."

John the Baptist is only the introduction, the preface. Wait until they hear the Word made flesh, Jesus. John is simply bringing greetings. He is a messenger. Jesus is the Messiah.

Sure, John is baptizing them, calling them to account and preaching prophetically. But he's just trying to get them ready. Jesus is coming soon, and they must clean up their act. All John has is water, but Jesus is coming with the Holy Spirit and fire. They haven't seen anything yet.

And John is clear on who he is. "I am not to be compared to him, and he is not to be compared to me. We are not even in the same category." John said he is not good enough to take care of Jesus' shoes, let alone stand in them. So, he told the crowd to make room: "Prepare the way of the Lord; make his paths straight."

John is just here to make an announcement. Salvation is on the way. Deliverance is near. John is baptizing the people, but Jesus is coming to clean house. But first he wants to be baptized by John, and John does it after some convincing.

Jesus is not above the message, but he must go down in the water too. He must fall in line. Yes, Jesus is Lord and Savior, Master and Messiah, Friend and Faithful One. But Jesus is also a human being, who stands at the end of John's line to be baptized. The greatest of all is now no better than any of us. Yet he has been set apart as God's beloved.

John is a part of this miraculous and mysterious encounter, but he is not running around boasting about his special baptisms. He isn't passing out business cards or setting up shop down by the river. He does not attempt to capitalize on the work of God. He does not split the baptism service into John's baptisms and Jesus' baptisms. Nor does he form a different service and name it "Greater St. John's Baptism."

John knows that baptism is at least a two-step process but likely more. There is a step he does not control. He can do nothing except that to which he has been called. He cannot pretend to be someone he's not. John knows that there is something in the water that transforms us and leaves a watermark. He reminds us that: if we behave as if we have completed the work of baptism by offering a towel and handing out a certificate; if we do not make room for Jesus who is just down the road but, on his way, to baptize with the Holy Spirit; if we attempt to quench the ongoing work of the Holy Spirit, then we are bearing witness to a watered-down gospel.

"You can go down a dry devil and come up a wet devil" is a joke about the efficacy of full immersion baptism. Though instituted by Christ himself and positioned as the means through which to enter the "kin-dom" of God,[12] the quip implies that a *baptizand* or candidate for baptism is somehow able to defy or reject the new life in Christ that the ritual is meant to symbolize.

Said in jest, it suggests that there are evils that persist despite baptismal "regeneration."[13]

Baptism is a re-enactment of the death, burial, and resurrection of Jesus.[14] While it is not a means of salvation, in Christian scripture it is often coupled with repentance. Peter said to a crowd in the Acts of the Apostles, "Repent and be baptized every one of you in the name of Jesus Christ so that your sins may be forgiven; and you will receive the gift of the Holy Spirit."[15] Peter's directive is referred to as "believer's baptism," usually reserved for persons who have reached the age of accountability for their personal confession of faith in Jesus as Savior and Lord.

Baptism is believed to be a means of spiritual re-entry into the world wherein believers are given a new humanity, a new way of being and belonging through Christian community. "Christianity means community through Jesus Christ and in Jesus Christ. No Christian community is more or less than this," Dietrich Bonhoeffer wrote in *Life Together.*[16] Also, persons were often given a Christian name during baptism to mark this transition. They were now children of God.

Some Christians refer to themselves as "born-again believers," which implies that their former way of life is dead to them. The Apostle Paul claimed that Jesus' disciples now lived for him: "From now on then, therefore, we regard no one from a human point of view; even though we once knew Christ from a human point of view, we know him no longer in that way. So, if anyone is in Christ, there is a new creation."[17] Baptism, a rite of passage, changed the way in which Christian believers related to each other. It seemingly had the power to transform the way they saw each other, no longer from "a human point of view" but in a way that was perhaps otherworldly.

Why then is the church in North America still segregated on Sunday mornings? Howard Thurman's question in *Jesus and the Disinherited* addressed this discrepancy:

> Why is it that Christianity seems impotent to deal radically, and therefore effectively, with the issues of discrimination and injustice on the basis of race, religion and national origin? Is this impotency due to a betrayal of the genius of the religion or is it due to a basic weakness in the religion itself?[18]

While it is presently justified as a necessary evil due to cultural differences and differences of opinion regarding worship style, the existence of the Black Church and the White Church is a literal sign of segregation—hanging over the North American church in judgment.

The segregated church is a byproduct of the sociopolitical construct of race traceable to Enlightenment thinkers' theories on human being and belonging, which ordered bodies according to their physical appearance. The concept actually "signifies and symbolizes social conflicts and interests by referring to different types of bodies."[19] This is in addition to the implications of American slavery, which attempted to dehumanize African people and re-create them as property. Not surprisingly, the baptism of African people who were enslaved was initially prohibited as European colonizers thought that it would manumit them.[20]

William Willimon asks, "What are we to do with a church that speaks to people on the basis of their gender or race, all the while baptizing them on the basis of Galatians 3:28?"[21] Not wanting to throw the church out with its baptism water, I come to this work through what Howard Thurman describes as a "creative encounter" and a process called "deconstructing," wherein I am breaking down race for analysis and theological scrutiny. "As a person, each of us lives a private life; there is a world within where for us the great issues of our lives are determined," Thurman writes in *The Creative Encounter*.[22] Race, white supremacy, and their progeny are the great issues of mine.

Take Me to the Water is a few sheets from my "working paper"[23] as I aim to strain Jesus' gospel of racialization and call the North American church to repentance for sins committed in support of a racialized worldview and the segregation of human beings. I am calling the church to live into its baptismal identity through the proclamation of the raceless gospel, because we're all God's children preparing for a coming "kin-dom." Anything less is a watered-down gospel not worth repeating or listening to on a Sunday morning.

This book is also my personal response to experiences that are not unique to racialized communities made to believe that light and dark, good and evil signify one's physical body. Like all the generations before me, I have experienced predation, harassment, and discrimination based on the sociopolitical construct of race. I remember a time when the invisible boundary got in front of and way ahead of me. The raceless gospel is my answer to this mistreatment, but it is also "my moral odyssey."[24] I had to go and prepare a place for me, free of white supremacy. It is "how I got over" while putting race in its place. It is how I heard Jesus calling me and when I was sure that he had changed my name.

Though I sometimes hear the voices of internalized racism, I hear more clearly now the voices of my ancestors declaring, "I am somebody!" Treat these slips of paper as notes on my deliverance, how I escaped "the race trap" and now raceless, free from all competing identities. I question race because I am a baptized believer, and it is my calling to discredit any word that attempts to create a hierarchy of being. The raceless gospel undermines the notion that if one's skin is "light enough," then she can be spared the double curse of being born "black and ugly" since Christians don't believe that Jesus died to save our skin.

While working to relocate identity outside of whiteness and its comparative identities, the raceless gospel is representative of a personal investment in self-determined worth and meaning outside of the dominating culture. Likewise, I am waving a white flag over socially-colored black bodies as the epic battle over evil, first as heathen and now suspect who fits the description of a criminal, continues to be wrongly waged against them. Africans and later African Americans have historically represented cosmic darkness tucked under their epidermis. Unfortunately, the church in North America has had a hand in all of this and is a part of its testimony.

Race is a conversion narrative that re-creates persons in these socially-colored images that come with pluses and minuses such as white privilege and oppression, socially-colored because, as pointed out by Henry Louis Gates Jr., "Who has seen a black or red person, a white, yellow or brown? These terms are arbitrary constructs, not reports of reality."[25] The works of David Roediger (*The Wages of Whiteness: Race and the Making of the American Working Class, Working Toward Whiteness: How America's Immigrants Became White*, and *Colored White: Transcending the Racial Past*), Ian Haney Lopez (*White by Law: The Legal Construction of Race*), and Nell Irvin Painter (*The History of White People*) document the history of this social arrangement of power and the forming of a new community called white, which denigrates African people, maligning their country of origin and changing their last names to those of their oppressors. Before the arrival of these immigrants, enslaved Africans were forced to deny their cultural linkage to the continent of Africa and forbidden to speak their languages and retain their ancestral names. They had been forcibly "baptized" during the Middle Passage and been reborn as racialized human beings. Their country of origin, ancestral heritage, and cultural identity were forcibly exchanged for the color black.

Thus, the raceless gospel is not to be confused with a colorblind lens or a post-racial vision of America. Instead, this baptismal pedagogy empowers us to see race as a hegemonic category and liberates us from these oppressive inventions so that we can live liberally in Jesus as a member of his body in anticipation of a "kin-dom" that is coming.[26] It also returns us to our countries of origin, our native lands, and roots us in the God whom notable theologian Paul Tillich calls the "Ground of Being." It is an opportunity to come home and to be right at home in your body.

Also, unlike the transcendent baptismal identity, racialized identities are temporal, "modern," with meanings that fluctuate as those who are socially-colored white change over time.[27] The proclamation of the raceless gospel, its acceptance and practical application after baptism, interrogates and nullifies the sociopolitical construct of race and its progeny. The raceless gospel for a "kin-dom" coming affirms the effects of baptismal identity and challenges structural inequality and systemic racism supported by racialized identities. Baptismal identity in Christ as defined in Galatians 3:27-28 and Colossians 3:9-11 submerges all other identities. Consequently, *Take Me to the Water* offers the raceless gospel expressed through baptismal identity as a catalyst for desegregating sacred space.

This book will draw from the work and witness of Howard Thurman, who guides my tongue as he offers both the required social analysis of segregation and the spiritual response of an integrated and fully authentic life—which is the work of the Christian faith in my view. I posit in this volume that the racializing of the Christian faith, evidenced by the various depictions of Jesus that hang in homes and sanctuaries—the idea that God is a white man—as well as the segregated church in North America, was never the intention of the gospel. Instead, it is proof of the coercion and co-option of the American empire and the church's outright rejection of the new community that Jesus created through his body and by the power of the Holy Spirit.

Positing the desegregation of sacred space as a practice of discipleship, I call attention to the segregated church, explain the meaning and significance of baptism and also the personal and social implications of a baptismal identity. Chapter 1 provides a historical overview of how the segregated North American church came to be and also definitions of race and its progeny as understood by anthropologists, historians, lawyers, and theologians. Chapter 2 examines the history of baptism, baptismal identity, the baptismal formula's implications for a just society, and the church's forgotten creed. Chapter 3 details the work and efficacy of baptism to challenge structural divisions within the North American church. In Chapter 4, I record my gleanings and what we can all draw from the water. The final chapter offers a summary that doubles as a benediction, a parting blessing as we re-enter the world with new eyes to see. Thus, it by no means the end of our learning.

Take Me to the Water does just that. You must decide to get in and fully immerse yourself in the work and witness of baptism, convicted that the old, racialized self is not a part of the new life with Christ. While reading this book, the water will start to trouble you and you may question what you've gotten yourself into. But that's only the beginning of the transformative work of the raceless gospel. I'll be waiting for you when you get out.

CHAPTER I

Troubled Water

Take me to the water
Take me to the water
Take me to the water
To be baptized

It all starts in the water. Christianity and American slavery proved an odd couple right from the beginning, despite its forced union for the economic exploitation of African people. Conversion of this "heathen" population was used as justification for their enslavement and got this ball and chain rolling. European human traffickers preferred their position as master over their identity as Christians. This decision would ultimately lead to the creation of the Black and White church. Consequently, any conversation about the history of Christianity in North America or its present condition as segregated and polarizing must include the institution of chattel slavery and baptismal freedom, which threatened the entire system and its hierarchy of identities.

In 1619, on the coast of the British colony Jamestown, Virginia, twenty African people—including at least three women—arrived and were treated as cargo. This was the beginning of American slavery. Nikole Hannah-Jones' *The 1619 Project: A New Origin Story* prefaces the work with a poem by Langston Hughes titled "American Heartbreak: 1619." He concludes,

> I am the American heartbreak—
> The rock on which Freedom
> Stumped its toe—
> The great mistake
> That Jamestown made
> Long ago.[28]

For Hughes and countless others, American slavery is viewed as *the* major misstep of a country that prides itself on being a democracy. Still, it is here that America, and likewise, the North American church got its start *and* started off on the wrong foot.

Hannah-Jones' book was not well-received by a group of historians due to her claim that America was founded on slavery and "anti-Blackness."[29] She believes it was the work of one paragraph, one sentence in particular that caused their dis-ease, writing: "Conveniently left out of our founding mythology is the fact that one of the primary reasons the colonists decided to declare their independence from Britain was because they wanted to protect the institution of slavery."[30] That group of historians didn't like the connection being made between slavery and the American Revolution.

But discomfort with the facts doesn't change them. The defiance of those colonists was also an expression of their faith. "When Protestant nations expanded across the Atlantic ... [they] redefined the relationship between slavery and Protestantism," writes Katherine Gerber in *Christian Slavery: Conversion and Race in the Protestant Atlantic World.*[31] Before the sociopolitical construct of race was invented, baptism would make all the difference.

Between the sixteenth and nineteenth centuries, Africans were kidnapped, traded for goods, and forced to render unpaid services during the European slave trade,[32] a global operation that transported some ten to twelve million Africans from diverse nations and differing tongues across the Atlantic Ocean to the Americas. It is estimated that two million died during the deadly voyage.

While he was not the first to offer an account of his experience as an enslaved person who also converted to Christianity, Olaudah Equiano was the first to write it himself. Published in 1789, *The Interesting Narrative of the Life of Olaudah Equiano* is widely regarded as the prototype of the slave narrative. Through his testimony, we learn of the atrocity of the Middle Passage, the brutality of the human traffickers, the suffering of those caught in the web of capitalist greed, the scenes of abuse on the ship's deck, and the stench of death below in the galley. While writing of his sister, whom he prays to see again and hopes will be spared of ill treatment, he recounts: "the violence of the African trader, the pestilential stench of a Guinea ship, the seasoning in the European colonies, [and] the lash and lust of a brutal and unrelenting overseer."[33] Equiano's account also disputed the European claim that African people were unable to write or represent their experiences through writing.

As to charges of uncleanness or the absence of religiosity that were often used to justify the enslavement of African people, Equiano compared his faith experience to that of the Jews and claimed they too practiced circumcision and ritual cleansing. He wrote, "I have before remarked that the natives of this part of Africa are extremely cleanly [sic]. This necessary habit of decency was with us a part of religion, and therefore we had many purifications and washings; indeed, almost as many, and used on the same occasion, if my recollection does not fail me, as the Jews."[34] He adds later that though they had no designated place for public worship, they were not without spiritual leaders.

After introducing the reader to himself and his native customs, Equiano shares his experience aboard the ship: "a multitude of black people of every description [were] chained together, everyone of their countenances expressing dejection and sorrow, I no longer doubted my fate; and, quite overwhelmed with horror and anguish, I fell motionless on the deck and fainted."[35] Perhaps he was experiencing what Orlando Patterson refers to as a "social death," the first in a series that began when European colonizers attempted to turn human beings into chattel property. Patterson writes, "Slavery, which on the level of secular symbolism was social death, became on the level of sacred symbolism spiritual death."[36] The mere awareness of the levels of loss was, for Equiano, physically overwhelming. So deadly was the voyage that the travel pattern of sharks that consumed African bodies—the corpses thrown overboard and the bodies of those who jumped to deliver themselves from subjugation—remains unchanged today.[37] Like the land, Africans were viewed as a natural resource to be used for the advancement of the world and its inhabitants.

It was a part of the natural order of things, the "Great Chain of Being,"[38] and for the European colonists, a necessity. Pro-slavery apologists argued for the enslavement of non-Europeans as a means of conversion, which was considered synonymous with civility. Being a Christian carried a measure of status and suggested that one possessed self-mastery. Conversion was the difference between the civilized and the heathen.

The European colonists, however, knew conversion and specifically baptism for Africans who they had enslaved would prove problematic. They knew "'they should, according to the laws of the British nation and the canons of the church' be freed (though) legally vague (it was) widely believed."[39] It could also be used as an argument for manumission.[40] The European colonists wanted quite literally to keep Jesus' gospel and baptismal freedom for themselves. Perhaps this is why for the first 120 years of American slavery, "little headway was made in converting the slave population to Christianity."[41] Instead, requests for laws preventing their freedom—though baptized believers—began in 1664 in Maryland with this appeal: "to draw up an Act obliging negroes to serve *durante vita*... for the prevencion of the damage Masters of such Slave must susteyne by such Slaves pretending to be Christ[e]ned [;] And soe pleade the law of England."[42] In addition to these laws being put in place, baptismal freedom as solely spiritual was made a part of the baptizand's catechism.

With no desire to lead them to Christ, European colonizers also complained that neither they nor the enslaved Africans had the time to offer or receive instruction. With a sunup-to-sundown work schedule and one day off to rest, plant, and tend to a small crop if permitted, visit with family and friends, and enjoy a bit of merriment, the Sabbath was ruled out. When the timing did work out, Africans who were enslaved were often required to recite a baptismal vow that ensured their continued enslavement before receiving this Christian rite of passage. Attributed to Francis Le Jau, a missionary to South Carolina with the Society for the Propagation of the Gospel, baptizands were instructed to confess the following:

> You declare in the presence of God and before this Congregation that you do not ask for the holy baptism out of any design to free yourself from the Duty and Obedience that you owe to your Master while you live, but merely for the good of Your Soul and to partake of the Graces and Blessings promised the members of the Church of Jesus Christ.[43]

The implications of baptism as offering an internal sameness and the sharing of Christlikeness were not conducive to the maintenance of the dynamic.

There was no mention of Galatians 3:27-28 or Colossians 3:9-11, wherein the power dynamics of culture, class, and gender are removed as baptized members join Christ's mystical body. However, there was the understanding that baptism changes one's social status. Consequently, the North American church became segregated "down by the riverside" at baptism. The first "whites only" sign was hung above the baptismal pool.

There was nothing redemptive or Christian about American slavery. As M. Shawn Copeland rightly pointed out in *Enfleshing Freedom; Body, Race and Being*:

> No Christian teaching has been more desecrated by slavery than the doctrine of the human person or theological anthropology. ... Three convictions central to the theological anthropology derive from Christian interpretation of this (i.e. Genesis 1-3) narrative: (1) that human beings, created in the image and likeness of God (imago Dei), have a distinct capacity for communion with God; (2) that human beings have a unique place in the cosmos God created; and, (3) that human beings are made for communion with other living beings. ... Slavery deformed these convictions. ... Slavery sought to displace God and thus, it blasphemed.[44]

European colonizers, who also claimed to be practicing Christians, created heretical hoops through which enslaved Africans and African Americans were to jump.

Before the enslaved could come to Jesus, they had to come to a few of their oppressor's conclusions as evidenced in the interview of James Smith in 1852 by Henry Bibb, who writes, "While he was a slave of this man, he became a convert to the Christian religion, and made application to the

Baptist Church one Sabbath-day to be admitted into the church and the ordinances of baptism: but the minister refused to have to do with him until he could see Br. Wright (his master), who was a member of the same church, about it."[45]

After the minister met with Smith's master, William Wright, who gave him permission to be baptized, Smith was examined by the preacher. He passed this initial examination but was then asked by William Wright these additional questions: "Do you feel as if you loved your master better than you ever did before, and as if you could do more work and do it better? Do you feel willing to bear correction when it is given you, like a good and faithful servant, without fretting, murmuring, or running away as has therefore been your practice? If so, it is an evidence that you are a good boy, and you may be baptized."[46]

It allows us to see the hypocrisies of American slavery, this cruel and unusual system of nation-building in which enslaved Africans were deemed second-class souls. Uprooted from their native land and prevented from speaking in their native language, every aspect of their lives was controlled to ensure their lifelong submission and obedience to European colonizers who re-created themselves as masters. The enslaved were denied the basic practice of theology as defined by St. Anselm, that is "faith seeking understanding." However, the denial was required for the machinations of this system of oppression to continue.

Against conversion and thus the rite of baptism, the European colonizers wanted quite literally to keep Jesus' gospel and baptismal freedom for themselves. Jemar Tisby writes in *The Color of Compromise*: "It had been a longstanding custom in England that Christians, being spiritual brothers and sisters, could not enslave one another. Yet the economy of the European colonies in North America depended more and more on slave labor."[47] Abolitionist evangelism could prove an enemy to their economic interests. Consequently, religion was used as a mechanism for control and the word "slave" took on an entirely new meaning.

In Romans 6, "slave" is used to separate people into two groups: "slaves to sin" and "slaves of righteousness."[48] In addition, enslavement is presented as spiritually beneficial for those who suffer through it and is coupled with Christ's own suffering.[49] "It was an act of mercy, the argument went, to enslave the body and free the soul from damnation," write Anne H. and Anthony B. Pinn in the *Fortress Introduction to Black Church History*.[50] There is also no law against owning a fellow believer in Christian scripture. It was, however, forbidden for a non-believer to own a Christian according to Justinian's *Code* and later the Church Council at Clichy in 626/7. The argument was taken up again in 743 at the Church Council at Estinnes and once more in the late eighth century at the Church Council at Meaux, where it was decided that Christians should only be sold to other Christians.[51] In America, the year was 1705.

Arguably, it was offered out of care and concern. The Virginia Slave Codes of 1705 states: "And for a further christian care and usage of all christian servants, *Be it also enacted*... That no negroes, mulattos, or Indians, although christians, or Jews, Moors, Mahometans, or other infidels, shall at any time, purchase any christian servant, nor any other, except of their own complexion, or such as are declared slaves by this act."[52] Here, Christianity and complexion are intermingled. The social-coloring[53] of skin, which will later be associated with the sociopolitical construct of race, is a determining factor as to who can be enslaved and who can oversee enslaving.

These European human traffickers had colonized in Jesus' name, calling on patron saints George and Santiago (James) for victory. Charged by the missionaries to also spread the gospel, they added cultural assimilation to the qualifications for conversion to Christianity. Likewise, Christianizing slaveholding would be no different, using the faith as its highest endorsement though chattel slavery was not its reference point and Jesus' point is made metaphorically.[54] Regeneration, being "born again,"[55] signified one's external appearance, the judgemnts based on race rather than the internal work of the Holy Spirit. The disposition of the heart was ultimately exchanged for "aesthetic" righteousness. Tisby says, "In European North America, Christianity became identified with the emerging concept of whiteness while people of color, including the indigenous peoples and Africans, became identified with unbelief."[56] Conversion had literally been given a face value.

Writing about the experiences of Morgan Godwyn, a minister who arrived in Virginia in the 1660s[57] to witness a kind of Christianity that refused to proselytize and discouraged the baptism of the enslaved Africans, Rebecca Anne Goetz made these connections:

> More shocking was the colonial link between being Christian and being English, and being black and being heathen. ... The colonial experience corrupted that understanding of Christianity. In the New World, Godwyn found, planters believed enslaved blacks were inherently incapable of becoming Christians. This notion apparently extended to the native people as well. ... [H]e was reacting against a trend he observed in the colony, one that separated people on the basis of their Christianity and associated Christianity with English descent and heathenism with Indian[58] or African

descent. By describing the "corrupt Custom" that rendered the enslaved people unable to be Christian, Godwyn exposed a feature of colonial life: the conflation of religious and racial categories. ...[59]

Christian, English, free, and *white* could be used interchangeably. Not until this time was enslavement or its justification based on physical features, namely skin color. The status of slave became racialized and codified into law during American slavery. Surprisingly, the editors of *A Mighty Baptism: Race, Gender, and the Creation of American Protestantism* do not include a single essay or section on baptism—with its only mention being in the introduction of the title of the book.[60] J. Cameron Carter's book, *Race: A Theological Account*, also makes no mention of baptism.

Yes, Christians in North America embedded racial categories into Christian identity. The North American church was founded on exclusion, with English settlers claiming the Christian identity for themselves only. They, along with their Danish and Dutch counterparts, found the conversion of the enslaved Africans to be "incompatible with slavery" because it would render them equals, children of God and thus, their siblings.[61] Once the oppressed started to become baptized believers, their oppressors could no longer identify with Christianity in the same way. Consequently, the latter felt they had to create a separate expression of the faith, a *white* Christianity. By racializing the gospel, the European colonizers had found a way to maintain power so as not to lose the Africans enslaved as chattel property. "Another gospel," white Christianity and the newly created white identity— which first appeared as a form of self-identification in 1680—would be used to shore up their newfound position of supremacy in the colonies.[62]

White and Christian had been used interchangeably and then synonymously. "Towards the end of the seventeenth century, Protestant slave owners gradually replaced the term 'Christian' with the word 'white' in their law books and in their vernacular. Scholars have long recognized that whiteness emerged from the protoethnic term 'Christian,'" writes Gerber.[63] According to Gerber, "Protestantism was gradually divorced from freedom in a piecemeal fashion, colony by colony. This shift was accompanied by the codification of racial slavery, as 'white' replaced 'Christian' in colonial taxonomy."[64] After making it a kind of religion, their domination was now explained as white supremacy.

To be sure, there is no biblical origin or biological basis for race. Frank M. Snowden Jr. made a tight case in *Before Color Prejudice: The Ancient View of Blacks*, writing that "the ancients did not fall into the error of biological racism; black skin color was not a sign of inferiority; Greeks and Romans did not establish color as an obstacle to integration in society; and ancient society was one that 'for all its faults and failures never made color the basis for judging a (person)." [65] Years later, in *Troubling Biblical Waters: Race, Class, and Family,* Cain Hope Felder wrote: "Today popular Christianity too easily assumes that modern ideas about race are traceable to the Bible… Centuries of European and Euro-American scholarship, along with a 'save the heathen blacks' missionary approach to Africans, have created these impressions." [66] Jamelle Bouie wrote in her essay, "The Enlightenment's Dark Side," that "it took the scientific thought of the Enlightenment to create an enduring racial taxonomy and the 'color-coded, white-over-black' ideology with which we are familiar." [67] But it must be noted that not everyone agreed. Some treated the theory of separate races of human beings as heresy because it called for separate origin stories known as *polygenesis,* which argues that only particular hominids reflect God's image and thus, each race had an individual and unrelated creation narrative.

This human identity project took "the setting aside of the metaphysical and theological scheme of things for a more logical description and classification that ordered humankind in terms of physiological and mental criteria based on observable 'facts' and tested evidence," as historian Ivan Hannaford wrote in *Race: The History of an Idea in the West.* [68] Michael Omi and Howard Winant rightly said that race "signifies and symbolizes social conflicts and interests by referring to different types of bodies." [69] Presbyterian minister Samuel Stanhope Smith even wrote a treatise, *Essays on the Causes of the Variety of Complexion and Figure* in 1787. [70] However, this is not to be confused with the social-coloring of skin being attributed to aesthetic sensibilities or defining sin as pointed out Gay L. Byron in *Symbolic Blackness and Ethnic Difference in Early Christian Literature.* It is only to point out again that physical differences were not attributed to race. Before American slavery, race referred to one's heredity and ancestry.

Race as a sociopolitical construct has been affirmed by the American Anthropological Association, which released this statement on May 17, 1998:

> Historical research has shown that the idea of "race" has always carried more meanings than mere physical differences; indeed, physical variations in the human species have no meaning except the social ones that humans put on them. Today scholars in many fields argue that "race" as it is understood in the United States of America was a social mechanism invented during the 18th century to refer to those populations brought together in colonial

America: the English and other European settlers, the conquered Indian peoples, and those peoples of Africa brought in to provide slave labor.

From its inception, this modern concept of "race" was modeled after an ancient theorem of the Great Chain of Being, which posited natural categories on a hierarchy established by God or nature. Thus "race" was a mode of classification linked specifically to peoples in the colonial situation.[71]

Race, racialized identities, and their progeny are unique to this system of oppression and the social, political, and theological mechanisms that keep the wheels turning.

Toni Morrison concludes in *Playing in the Dark: Whiteness and the Literary Imagination*: "Race has become metaphorical—a way of referring to and disguising forces, events, classes, and expressions of social decay and economic division far more threatening to the body politic than biological 'race' ever was. Expensively kept, economically unsound, a spurious and useless political asset in election campaigns, racism is as healthy today as it was during the Enlightenment."[72] Race is a tool used to pit the majoritized and minoritized against each other, to make certain segments of the American population the problem. First, there was "the Negro Problem," "the Indian Problem," and "Yellow Peril." Today, there is the immigration debate and the feared "browning of America."

Isabel Wilkerson describes American race as an "unseen skeleton" that holds these arguments in place. In *Caste: The Origins of our Discontents*, she writes: "Like other old houses, America has an unseen skeleton, a caste system that is central to its operation as are the studs and joists that we cannot see in the physical building we call home. Caste is the infrastructure of our divisions. It is the architecture of human hierarchy, the subconscious code of instructions for maintaining, in our case, a four-hundred-year-old social order. Looking at caste is like holding the country's X-ray up to the light."[73] Race makes America a "house of bondage."[74]

Charles W. Mills describes white supremacy as "the unnamed political system that has made the modern world what it is today." Consequently, this is not by happenstance, but it has been agreed to and agreed on time and again. Mills calls it "the racial contract," writing that "the peculiar contract to which I am referring, though based on the social contract tradition that has been central to Western political theory, is not a contract between everybody ('we the people'), but between just the people who count, the people who are really people ('we the white people'). So, it is a Racial Contract."[75] We need only to look at the numbers and who is allowed to come across the water and the border.

Socially-colored is a description I coined to denote the fact that human beings are not physically colored beige (mixed race), black, brown, red, yellow, and white. So-called white people remain the racialized majority because of laws passed by the U.S. government to include the Indian Removal Act of 1830, the Chinese Exclusion Act of 1882, the Immigration Act of 1924 (which included the Asian Exclusion Act and the National Origins Act), and the Undesirable Aliens Act of 1929. Ian Haney Lopez writes about the legal construction of race in *White by Law*: "… law constructs race at every level: changing the physical features borne by people in this country, shaping the social meanings that define races, and rendering concrete privileges and disadvantages justified by racial ideology."[76] The differences socially prescribed and the subsequent power dynamics were legalized. David Roediger, who has written a series of books on whiteness, points out in *Working Towards Whiteness: How America's Immigrants Became White* that "Race clearly defined the disabilities of the excluded Chinese workers, Jim Crowed African Americans, American Indians confined to reservations, and Puerto Ricans and Filipino subjects denied self-government."[77] Race is a numbers game.

James Baldwin called that which has been used to justify these crimes against the community a "curtain." There is much that is hidden behind it and much to be revealed once it is drawn back. Baldwin wrote in "White Man's Guilt," an essay for *Essence* magazine:

> The American curtain is color. White men have used this word, this concept to justify unspeakable crimes and not only in the past but in the present. One can measure very neatly the white American's distance from his conscience—from himself—by observing the distance between white America and black America. One has only to ask oneself who established this distance, who is the distance designed to protect, and from what is this distance designed to offer protection?[78]

Baldwin does the work of the baptismal identity, questioning race, place, and social positioning.

As members of one another, we must not only examine ourselves but also the system that keeps these oppressions going. Brian Bantum writes in *The Death of Race:*

> Race is a system, an intuition, a systemic reflex that seeks to decipher who can use who. It is an imaginative frame that justifies the death of the Native and the violence of the colonist, the deportation of the Mexican worker

and the citizenship of the Irish refugee. Race is a way of resisting difference by violently determining which differences matter. Race is about power, sovereignty, and how words can become enfleshed, part of our daily, bodily lives, shaping who we are.[79]

Today, race is also used to justify the continued segregation of the North American church.

Christian believers often say there are cultural distinctions and the worship styles of Europeans and African Americans differ. However, linguistic and cultural barriers were also offered as justification for the latter's lack of receptivity to the gospel. Further, there exists a Black and White church in North America because of the social, political, and theological implications of American slavery, namely the European colonizers' view that their power over bodies racialized as black and forcibly enslaved carried over to their "non-white" souls.[80] This racist paternalism meant that African and indigenous people were unworthy of and unable to accept the Christian faith unless European colonizers' "civilized" and subordinated them. This produced a "two-ness," a double-mindedness for the European colonizers and a double-consciousness[81] for Africans and later African Americans. In his *Narrative of the Life of Frederick Douglass*, Douglass names it plainly, writing,

> What I have said respecting and against religion, I mean strictly to apply to the slaveholding religion of this land, and with no possible reference to Christianity proper; for between the Christianity of this land, and the Christianity of Christ, I recognize the widest possible difference—so wide, that to receive one as good, pure, and holy, is of necessity to reject the other as bad, corrupt, and wicked. To be the friend of one, is of necessity to be the enemy of the other. I love the pure, peaceable, and impartial Christianity of Christ: I therefore hate the corrupt, slaveholding, women-whipping, cradle-plundering and hypocritical Christianity of this land. Indeed, I can see no reason, but the most deceitful one, for calling the religion of this land Christianity. I look upon it as the climax of all misnomers, the boldest of all frauds, and the grossest of all libels.[82]

Unwilling to let go of the superior power they coveted, the separateness afforded by this system and the exclusivity of being an oppressor, European American colonizers created another set of categorical identities and a community of faith that was antithetical to that of Christianity. Black liberation theology was created in direct response to slaveholding religion. It produced what Dwight N. Hopkins called the "two faces of Protestantism and American Culture," as described in *Down, Up, and Over: Slave Religion and Black Theology.*

> ... the Puritans sailed not to break with old Europe, but to bring about the logic and fullest extent of a hegemonic Protestantism and cultural civilization. That is why they named their colonial settlements New Haven, New Canaan, New Netherlands, New York, and Cambridge. Unfortunately, those bold pioneers brought the same view of blacks as demonic, evil, inferior, and sinful that their European mother churches had propagated in instinct, language, and symbol. The seeds of religious freedom, congregational democracy, and covenantal metaphor would grow to mean a rationalization for the development of a system of white skin privileges.[83]

The segregation of the North American church did not occur by happenstance but began the moment European Protestants positioned themselves as the go-between God and other nationalities for relationship.

Their practice of discipleship and especially evangelism proved hypocritical beyond comparison. Not all who heard the gospel accepted it, but for those who were receptive, the compromising position of the Christian oppressor was viewed as an obstacle and a source of complaint even for missionaries.[84] Commissioned to go and make disciples, European colonizers refused for fear of losing the Africans they enslaved as chattel property. Freedom in Christ or bondage for life, these slaveholding Christians chose to offer the latter as an expression of the faith.

Consequently, the "hush harbors" and "brush harbors," known as the "invisible institution," were entered by Africans who were enslaved to "steal away to Jesus" as an act of faith and to discern their life's meaning outside of the self-serving interpretations of scripture that justified their perpetual bondage, made possible by the colonizing version of Christianity. Even their forms of worship had been demonized: handclapping, foot patting, dancing, and drumming. (An Africanism or African retention, drumming was outlawed when it was discovered that the instrument was used to communicate information and instructions.) The Christianity offered by the European slaveholder sought only to maintain their oppressive condition. Quite naturally, these people, mostly from West Africa, came with their own faith traditions—Christianity, Islam, and African traditional religion—and were not without the ability to engage in theological inquiry.

Rarely permitted to gather in groups of more than two or three for fear of rebellion or escape, the enslaved Africans were not permitted to read and consequently to learn about the Christian faith apart from the instruction of a slaveholding preacher or an enslaved preacher who had been approved by the European enslaver. Not only were their bodies controlled, but this also was an attempt to govern their thoughts and to ensure that even after hearing the gospel, they acted according to the laws of their "earthly master."[85]

Harsh laws were enacted and penalties given for those who attempted to educate enslaved Africans, as their illiteracy supported their limited agency and bodily autonomy. In fact, the General Assembly of the Commonwealth of Virginia met on April 7, 1831, and made this declaration:

> *Be it further enacted,* That all meetings of free negroes or mulattoes, at any school-house, church, meeting-house or other place for teaching them reading or writing, either in the day or night, under whatsoever pretext, shall be deemed and considered as an unlawful assembly; and any justice of the county or corporation, wherein such assemblage shall be, either from his own knowledge, or on the information of others, of such unlawful assemblage or meeting, shall issue his warrant, directed to any sworn officer or officers, authorising him or them, to enter the house or houses where such unlawful assemblage or meeting may be, for the purpose of apprehending or dispersing such free negroes or mulattoes, and to inflict corporal punishment on the offender or offenders, at the discretion of any justice of the peace, not exceeding twenty lashes.[86]

In addition, European Americans found in the assembly for the purpose of instructing would be fined fifty dollars and could face up to sixty days in prison. If they were being compensated for their instruction, these teachers and all those who were involved in the contract for the assembly of enslaved persons would be fined no less than ten dollars and no more than one hundred dollars.

Such regulations were intended to control the spiritual meaning and social implications of their Christian conversion. Christianity was good for the enslaved Africans' self-esteem, which proved problematic for those who wanted to keep them in their place of perpetual bondage. It reminded them of their "somebodiness." Consequently, their relationship with God was treated as a third wheel that would ruin the chances of the European oppressor's continued advances. The teachings of Jesus did not support their mistreatment or the conditions of American slavery. Not only did the enslaved belong to God, but they also belonged to each other as members of Christ's body.

Albert J. Raboteau, in his book *Slave Religion: The "Invisible Institution" in the Antebellum South*, records a complaint about the effects of religious instruction: "George Ross, minister of Emmanuel Church in New Castle,

Delaware, explained that the one reason for the 'general indifference' of even churchgoing planters to the instruction of their slaves was 'the untoward haughty behavior of those Negroes who had been admitted into the Fellowship of Christ's Religion.'"[87] He writes later of another preacher, "Rev. Charles Martyn, of South Carolina, complained that some baptized slaves 'became lazy and proud, entertaining too high an opinion of themselves, and neglecting their daily labor.'"[88] Again and again, the case is made for the incompatibility of Christianity with human subjugation.

Eventually, the European colonizers loosened their reigns, and enslaved Africans and African Americans were permitted to gather on Sundays. It wasn't long before they saw themselves in Christian scripture, specifically in the Exodus narrative, which stood in stark contradiction with the sermons they had heard on the plantation and that focused on obeying their master and mistress. This liberation theology can be heard in the chorus: "Go down, Moses, Way down in Egypt's Land. Tell ol' Pharaoh, Let my people go." The Israelites' deliverance from Egyptian slavery became a prophecy for their own.

Polly, an enslaved African American woman, shared her experience with the dueling theologies: "We poor creatures have need to believe in God, for if God Almighty will not be good to us someday; why were we born? When I heard of his delivering his people from bondage, I know it means the poor African."[89] Despite this incredible theological gap between them, the two groups worshipped together. The revivals of the 1700s had yielded a high number of new converts. The dramatic preaching and high energy of the services along with the immediacy of conversion apart from the long process required for baptism proved effective.[90]

The revivals led by Baptists and Methodists had brought African and European American Christians together, but the American Revolution would separate them again with questions over slavery. How could American colonists fight for freedom from British oppression, claiming their natural rights, while participating in, supporting, and sustaining the oppression of Africans and African Americans? Petitions pointing out the blatant hypocrisy were submitted to the government of several colonies but largely ignored. Meanwhile, the outdoor gathering of the faithful for revival tent meetings continued.

Both denominations initially took a stance against slavery, strongly condemning it and forbidding their members and ministers from participating. In 1770, 1783, and 1784, the Methodist General Conferences of clergy and lay leaders strongly condemned slavery. And in 1789, the General Committee of Virginia Baptists "condemned slavery as a 'violent deprivation of the rights of nature and inconstant with a republican government.'"[91] The Baptists would hold the antislavery position, while opposition from the South remained. The Methodists decided that rather than speak as a group, the issues should be handled individually, so in 1785 they suspended its enforcement.

Nevertheless, the denominations had begun licensing African Americans to preach who, in turn, began to interpret the Bible through the lens of their experience. It was a part of the attraction. Melville Herskovits writes in *The Myth of the Negro Past:*

> [T]here was a strong attraction of the slaves for the Baptist church because they were given greater participation in religious exercises. ... There was also greater liberality among the Baptists in giving Negroes permission to preach while also in addition the Baptist method of administering communion was not calculated to discriminate against them. Finally, the mode of baptism among the Baptists satisfied the desire of the Negro for the spectacular.[92]

While there were certainly instances of persecution, with African American preachers being arrested and whipped for holding "illegal meetings," they were allowed to form their own churches, which were permitted to hold services during the day in addition to other conditions and restrictions.

Henry H. Mitchell shares in *Black Church Beginnings: The Long-Hidden Realities of the First Years* that the churches gathered under the supervision of socially-colored white people who, in some cases, formed committees that chose the pastor for the African American members.[93] They were separate but not free of the "white gaze" and its brutality. The First African Church of Savannah, led by Andrew Bryan, was organized in 1773, making it the nation's oldest African American-led church in North America. For those who continued worshiping with their European American siblings, their presence did not ease the fears of their oppressors who thought that African Americans in leadership positions and in charge of organizations would upset the order of things as established by American slavery.

These churches were separate but not independent of the arbitrary authority of socially-colored white people. Raboteau states in *Canaan Land* that "Between 1790 and 1820, Black Episcopalians, Methodists, Baptists, and Presbyterians founded churches and struggled with church leaders to exercise varying degrees of independence from white control."[94] Mechal Sobel offers additional insight, recording that "Whereas white Baptists in Georgia sought to infiltrate and dominate black churches, those in Virginia... chose [as required by law after the Nat Turner Rebellion] to maintain black churches as branches."[95] This was done to surveil and control both their social and spiritual lives.

While African Americans gathered to worship God, they were also not permitted, in many cases, to do so without paying for their unsolicited surveillance by European Americans. Mitchell makes it clear, writing,

> Whether whites exited mixed congregations and formed their own separate congregation, the black group was always thought of as the church's mission, subordinate to the sponsoring church. This arrangement was inevitable because of the legal requirement for white sponsors and guarantors. Without such, the government prohibited blacks from gathering for mass worship at all. In most cases, the separation of congregations was supposedly amicable, but in every case, the black congregation had no choice but to accept 'assistance' and continued supervision of a pastoral nature.[96]

Mitchell says of the separation of African and European American Christians: "It was not just plain and simple racial antipathy or prejudice. It was also the differences in the three 'c's' of class, culture, and control."[97] *White* Christianity and its believers' inability to believe and behave in ways that did not affirm the hierarchical identities of American slavery while in church and at worship continued to be a problem.

But in 1794, Richard Allen and Absalom Jones had had enough. After learning that they, along with other African American members of St. George's, were expected to sit in the back of the balcony, the men refused. After the prayer was rendered, they walked out of the church. In the same year, Allen founded Bethel African Methodist Episcopal Church in Philadelphia, Pennsylvania, and the African Methodist Episcopal Church, the first African American denomination, in 1816 for which he was elected its bishop. Absalom Jones was called to serve St. Thomas African Methodist Episcopal Church in 1794.[98] Other African American denominations were formed, with activism as the hallmark of the African American religious experience and the Black Church tradition.[99]

While African Americans were forming denominations, the Methodist and Baptist denominations among others were splitting over whether to practice Christianity or slavery. The Methodist Church would split in 1844. The Baptists followed a year later, with the Southern Baptists supporting slavery and the Northern Baptists against it. The churches separated before the states did, as the Civil War did not begin until 1861. The North American church split over slavery and has yet to reckon with it fully, which is why it remains segregated on Sunday mornings.

Created in response to *white* Christianity and white supremacist terrorism, the Black Church is the moral compass and prophetic voice of American Christianity. Anne and Anthony Pinn say of the religious institution:

> Obscure in origin, secret in development, rich and complex in its flowering, the oldest and most influential institution in African American life remains the Black Church. In fact, the African American engagement with Christianity has not only shaped, consoled, and empowered a people caught in slavery for more than two centuries, it has also captured and emboldened their spirit in such a way as to engender profound social change across all of America.[100]

It also serves as a sacred and safe space for bodies racialized as black in a white supremacist society, "free from interference by the white community,"[101] and offers a means of relating to God on terms not dictated by the sociopolitical construct of race and its progeny. The Black Church exists in an effort to decolonize its members' bodies, to affirm that we are all God's children, and to have "a little talk with Jesus" without being interrupted by an oppressor.

Joseph Washington summarizes the symbiotic relationship between the African American-led church and its community, writing,

> In the beginning was the black church, and the black church was with the black community, and the black church was the black community. The black church was in the beginning with the black people; all things were made through the black church, and without the black church was not anything made that was made. In the black church was life; and the life was the light of the black people.[102]

The Black Church would continue to be the social, political, and religious hub in the 1950s and 60s, the community's center and the place where African Americans organized to protest for their civil rights.

Still segregated in secular and sacred spaces, the organizers of the Civil Rights Movement nonviolently demonstrated throughout the South until buses, cemeteries, drinking fountains, hospitals, the military, schools, and universities were desegregated. There were kneel-ins to integrate Southern churches but to no effect. Both African and European Americans attempted to enter segregated sacred spaces but were prevented, often stopped at the door by the church's lay leaders. When America was being pulled in two different directions, some Christians were moved to provide moral clarity and a clarion call to repent and reconcile.

Stephen R. Haynes reports in *The Last Segregated Hour*: "These Sunday morning protests occurred at churches affiliated with every major Christian denomination, involved representatives from key civil rights organizations, and occupied a vital place in the minds of movement spokespersons and strategists."[103] Members, for and against segregation, took sides, often spiritually bypassing the real issue with claims of "liberalism." Haynes sees through it and makes this point: "These official memories persist because they conceal wounds inflicted on institutions that claim a moral identity. Since modern organizations do not claim such identities, they are rarely compelled to deny or justify their racist histories."[104] It is a traumatic experience for which the church in North America has not recovered, which is why it remains segregated.

In 2012, the National Congregations Study reported that eight in ten churches remain segregated; the numbers had not varied much in a follow-up conducted in 2018.[105] Baptist churches specifically remain divided into Southern and Northern expressions with the Southern Baptist Convention and the American Baptist Churches, USA, formerly known as the Northern Baptist Convention. In 2014, the Pew Research Center found that "while about eight-in-ten American congregants still attend services at a place where a single racial or ethnic group comprises at least eighty percent of the congregation, one-in-five now worship in congregations where no single racial or ethnic group predominates in such a way."[106] Segregation, which began with American slavery and the distinction between the "civilized" and the "heathen," today is racialized and faithfully divides socially-colored black and white Christians.

Mystic-theologian Howard Thurman wrote *Luminous Darkness: A Personal Interpretation of the Anatomy of Segregation and the Ground of Hope* during the struggle for integration. On the dynamics of power that are at work and the social positioning of color-coded bodies, he notes: "Segregation gives rise to an immoral exercise of power of the strong over the weak, that is to say, advantage over disadvantage. ... Segregation is at once one of the most blatant forms of moral irresponsibility. The segregated persons are out of bounds, are outside of the magnetic field of ethical concern. It is always open season."[107] Regarding the internal agreement that America's citizens must make, Thurman says, "In a free society, no law can endure unless it is accepted in the hearts of men."[108] He describes segregation as a pattern, and it is no doubt woven into the fabric of American society.[109]

In addition, Thurman defines, in my estimation, the racialized identity as "becom(ing) persons by an other-than-self reference which is other persons."[110] This distinction is critical for Christian who are divesting themselves of racialized identities—that is beige (mixed race), black, brown, red, yellow, and white—as part of accepting their baptismal identity as expressed in Colossians 3:10-11 and Galatians 3:27-28.[111] It is important to note that whiteness needs these other social colors to exist, as race is a color-coded hierarchy.

As James Baldwin said, white supremacism is "the nigger we (socially-colored white people) invent." The invention is depicted in Flannery O'Connor's "Artificial Nigger," as explained by Toni Morrison in *The Origin of Others*. She writes, "This story is a carefully rendered description of how and why blacks are so vital to a white definition of humanity."[112] Understanding the rationale for these socially constructed identities is critical to our understanding of segregation and the transformative power of a baptismal identity.

Thurman also describes how to keep its pseudo-justifications from impacting his inner being. He writes in *Luminous Darkness*, "As I look back on those days, I never gave to the way of living demanded of me by my environment, the inner sanction of my spirit. I gave to it what may be called the sanction of strategy. There was a place in me untouched by these pressures of my life."[113] He speaks of a deep, internal form of resisting and refusing to internalize racialized and segregated meanings for his life.

We hear this same kind of internal activism in the writings of James Baldwin. It is the working out of one's deliverance, one's salvation from the tentacles of race to ensure that there is a place for one to simply be. In "The White Problem" he writes, "Later on, one begins to discover, with great pain, and very much against one's will, that whatever it is you want, what you want, at bottom, must be to become yourself: there is nothing else to want."[114] It is in examining the church's work and witness to include its complicity in sins against humanity, specifically their understanding of human identity, being, and belonging. Baldwin continues, "The Christian church in this country is a very popular institution. But this has always been a racist institution, and we take this as immoral."[115] Consequently, the internal work begins with those given charge to lead our souls.

The most notable leader of the Civil Rights Movement, Martin Luther King Jr., named what all North American Christians knew to be true. In 1963, King remarked, "It is appalling that the most segregated hour of Christian America is 11 o'clock on Sunday morning." But he also provided a charge: "The Philosophy of Christianity is strongly opposed to the underlying philosophy of segregation. Therefore, every Christian is confronted with the basic responsibility of working courageously for a non-segregated society. The task of conquering segregation is an inescapable must confronting the Christian Churches."[116] This is the work of North American Christians, who still suffer from the rippling effects of an ancestral and generational betrayal of baptismal identity and its efficacy to rid our society of segregation.

Separate but equal on Sunday mornings, the North American church has yet to emerge as a baptized believer in the "kin-dom"[117] of God that is coming. My conviction is that the raceless gospel expressed through baptismal identity can act as a catalyst for desegregating sacred space. But the water must trouble baptized believers who come up and re-enter a world that does not treat everyone equally. It is going to take time, and we will likely need to wade in the water.

CHAPTER 2

Wading in the Water

Wade in the water
Wade in the water, children
Wade in the water
God's gonna' trouble the water

We are all in the same boat, caught in the storms of life with a Savior who takes naps at the most inopportune times it would seem. Our experience with him is no different than that of the first disciples. "He is the same yesterday, today, and forever."[118]

For us, it feels like the boat is about to capsize and Jesus yawns, stretches, and turns over. Water is getting into the boat, and Jesus is fluffing his pillow. We are getting seasick, and Jesus is getting more comfortable. We are putting on life vests, and he is pulling on his sheet. We are sending out S.O.S. signals, and Jesus is snoring. "Wake up, Jesus!"

This story of a sleepy-headed Savior is recounted in the gospels of Matthew, Mark, and Luke. But Jesus should be tired. In Mark's gospel, the boat is first a podium. Jesus stands in it to teach the people who are seated at the shoreline. It is discipleship by the sea.

Jesus has taught parables on the sower, the growing seed, and the mustard seed. He is understandably exhausted. The boat then acts as a kind of tour bus. Jesus leaves the crowd behind and thinking his work is done, lies down to take a nap. But the lesson has not taken root in the disciples. There is more work, more teaching, more leading by example that he must do.

And true to our human form, Jesus can never do enough. He always has to prove himself to them and to us. He could have just preached his best sermon, led city-wide revivals, fed thousands, delivered the oppressed, healed the sick, stopped funeral processions, dumbfounded the Pharisees, and caused some people to question their day job. And the fact is that he did. Still, there is a question of his care and commitment. Because Jesus is not even as good as his last miracle. While it may have been a showstopper, he is only as good as what he is doing for us right now.

We are aware of his track record, but right now it sounds like a broken record. We have heard all that before. What are you going to do now, Jesus? Water on my feet and rising fast, I need you to get up and do something.

The raindrops keep falling on my head. I need you to stop this, to make this storm go away. The disciples are talking to Jesus as if he needs a wake-up call.

Have you ever been in a storm and felt as if Jesus was sleeping right through it, as if he didn't care about what you were experiencing? Have you ever yelled at God, questioned God's presence when trouble comes? "Teacher, do you not care that we are perishing?"[119] We asked Jesus to take the wheel, but it seems that he is asleep at it.

Though Jesus saved us who were "sinking deep in sin," we do not trust him in a storm. When the tide turns, so do we. Because what we are experiencing has more credibility. Our trust, our hope, our faith is thrown overboard—every person for themself.

You know how the story ends. The disciples yell at Jesus and in turn, Jesus yells at the storm. He tells the storm to shut up, to be quiet, to be still. And the storm knows who is talking to it, but it is clear the disciples do not know who they are talking to: "Who then is this, that even the wind and the sea obey him?"[120]

If you have not learned already, Jesus does not move when we want him to. He has his own pace and his own way of doing things. The disciples learned this that day on the boat. He has to teach the same lesson to Mary.

In the gospel of John, her brother Lazarus has been dead three days. She and her sister Martha had called Jesus long before then. "Where were you, Jesus? I know that you got my message. You're late. If you had arrived sooner, Lazarus would still be alive."

And she's right: Jesus extended his stay. Mary and Martha are pacing the floor outside of Lazarus' room, and Jesus is seemingly dragging his feet. They are in a race against time but Jesus is, on the face of it, wasting time. Jesus loved Lazarus but not enough to leave, to stop what he was doing. *The sisters' emergency is not Jesus' emergency.*

Facing down death threats, he goes against the advice of his disciples[121] to fulfill Mary's request. It makes no difference to Mary and Martha. For all that Jesus does, he never does enough. For all that he gives, Jesus is always coming up short. Mary's words shortchange him to be sure. Like the disciples in the boat, she questions Jesus' concern for her family. Because she "knows" Jesus, she thinks she *knows* Jesus.

And this is why I love Jesus. Because he sings the blues of all hometown heroes, all local legends, all seers who are given visions for a time to come: "Prophets are not without honor, except in their own hometown and among their own kin, and in their own house."[122] There is something lost in familiarity, in proximity, in their closeness to Christ. Recognizable, they are unable to see who he really is. Jesus is right at home and with his own. And here's the sad part: "Jesus wasn't able to do much of anything there—he laid hands on a few sick people and healed them, that's all,"[123] Mark says.

Because recognition is not revelation. What you see is not what you get with Jesus.

This familiarity causes forgetfulness, a self-serving amnesia. Mary has forgotten who she is talking to. She thinks that Jesus' hands are too short to box with Death, that he cannot reach beyond the grave. Mary is talking to Jesus and Jesus, in turn, talks to God and then Lazarus: "Lazarus come out."[124] Jesus doesn't even speak to Death. Death is not addressed or even included in the conversation. Why? Because Jesus is the resurrection and the life.[125]

And for all the stories told about Jesus and the sermons that follow, we still do not realize that we are in the same boat, that nothing we experience in life or death can rock it. Because Jesus is in the boat, and he is "the captain of our souls." Jesus can come from anywhere at any time, with sleep in his eyes or a bounty on his head and stop it.

All the time, Jesus is rescuing and resurrecting. He is our lifeguard on duty and the only one who can interrupt a conversation with Death. William Willimon wrote in *Why Jesus?* that "Jesus is God's rescue operation. God's risky reach toward us and God's loving embrace of us, here, now, so that he may have us forever."[126]

We ask the same question when we think of the people Jesus saves. "Why, Jesus?" Still, the Apostle Paul's bloody hands are used to extend the call to salvation. In 2 Corinthians 12, Paul is addressing questions about spiritual gifts. For him, they are all the same. They all come from the "same Lord," "same God," "same Spirit."[127] Different gifts, but they are all the same. Many members, but none of them are better than the gift of unity in Christ's body.

"For just as the body is one and has many members, and all the members of the body, though many, are one body, so it is with Christ,"[128] Paul said. No matter our differences, there is unity in the diversity of our gifts. Just like the body, our members serve different functions, but they serve one body. No matter your gifts and no matter how many members, there is none larger than the life of Christ. No minority or majority, we all come together to form his body.

Because there is just one: one Spirit, one body of Christ, one Savior who gave his life so that we might live eternally. It all boils down to, comes down to, comes back to Jesus. And no one knows the way. It is a tight squeeze, this narrow way. We are all "baptized into one body."[129]

Now then, our old life is dead in the water. The life we once lived, we live no longer. This is the gospel of Jesus Christ. Once baptized, our lives are fully submerged, fully hidden, fully surrendered to his. Thus, the Christian is never out of the water. Jesus said, "Rivers of living water will brim and spill out of the depths of anyone who believes in me this way."[130]

Rachel Held wrote in *Searching for Sunday: Loving, Leaving, and Finding the Church*, "In the ritual of baptism, our ancestors acted out the bizarre truth of the Christian identity: We are people who stand totally exposed before evil and death and declare them powerless against love. There's nothing normal about that. But we try to make it just that. The world is chanting, 'Live and let live.' The markets are selling 'your best life now.' And the message of the gospel and the call of Christ's disciple is death, a lifelong funeral procession: 'If any want to become my followers, let them deny themselves and take up their cross and follow me.'"[131]

Because life with Christ leads to death. Morbid, it is his message. Sad, it is our salvation and is one of the greatest reversals proclaimed in the gospel: to die to self is to live in Christ, to trust that God has something better than this world has to offer, a "kin-dom" rather than this burned-out Eden. *William Willimon* says it well:

> We may come singing, "Just as I Am," but we will not stay by being our same old selves. The needs of the world are too great, the suffering and pain too extensive, the lures of the world too seductive for us to begin to change the world unless we are changed, unless conversion of life and morals becomes our pattern. The status quo is too alluring. It is the air we breathe, the food we eat, the six-thirty news, our institutions, theologies, and politics. The only way we shall break its hold on us is to be transferred to another dominion, to be cut loose from our old certainties, to be thrust under the flood and then pulled forth fresh and newborn. Baptism takes us there.[132]

This is what John the Baptist was preaching about, "proclaiming a baptism of repentance for the forgiveness of sins."[133] Repent, change your ways, and get washed up for the kingdom.[134] And before you tout your gifts and flash your cultural credentials, Jesus was baptized. What's good enough for the Savior is good enough for us.

We're all in the same boat, "a watery grave." Like the church at Corinth, we are encouraged to take it all in, "all made to drink of one spirit,"[135] to drink from the same cup Jesus offered his disciples: "Can you drink the cup I must drink, or be baptized with the baptism with which I must be baptized?"[136] Willimon continues, "[Jesus'] message is not the simple one of (John) the Baptist, 'Be clean.' Jesus' word is more painful— 'Be killed.'... The chief analogy of baptism is not the water that washes but the flood that drowns." So, what can a storm do? If the grave cannot hold you, what do you have to fear?

Get out of the boat because you didn't join a church: you entered a body of water.

No matter how you say it, baptism or *baptizo* for the Greeks, there's something about the water, specifically baptismal water right from the start, as evidenced in the early Christian community. After Peter's sermon in the book of Acts or the Acts of Peter and Paul, as some scholars describe it, those first converts wanted to act on the message.[137] Peter responded, "Repent and be baptized everyone one of you in the name of Jesus Christ so that your sins may be forgiven; and you will receive the gift of the Holy Spirit. For the promise is for you, for your children, and for all who are far away, everyone whom the Lord our God calls to him."[138] Peter cast a net wide and testified that this message was for everyone of his day and for generations to come.

In Acts 8, while Saul was busy persecuting the church, Philip was preaching in Samaria. His ministry included the healing of persons paralyzed and lame and deliverance for those possessed by "unclean spirits."[139] But he was not the only show in town. Simon was a magician and while Philip had put a smile on people's faces, this crowd had also been Simon's audience. The gospel message did the trick, however: "But when they believed Philip, who was proclaiming the good news about the kingdom of God and the name of Jesus Christ, they were baptized, both men and women. Even Simon himself believed. After being baptized, he stayed constantly with Philip and was amazed when he saw the signs and great miracles that took place."[140] Baptism was immediate and without instruction. It sealed the deal and was proof of their new relationship as family members.

In Acts 9, Saul has a theophany that marked his conversion experience to Christianity. He sees a bright light and falls to the ground. Then Jesus asks him directly, "Saul, Saul, why do you persecute me?"[141] When Saul gets up, he cannot see and so is led by his traveling companions to a man named Ananias, whom Saul had been instructed to meet through a vision. Saul's reputation preceded him and initially, Ananias rightly refused to see him.

Ananias knew Saul's identity, but God knew who Saul would be. Luke testified to this, writing, "But the Lord said to him, 'Go, for he is an instrument whom I have chosen to bring my name before Gentiles and kings and before the people of Israel; I, myself, will show him how much he must suffer for the sake of my name."[142] Saul would cross enemy lines. There was no need for retribution, so Ananias laid his hands on "brother Saul" and the scales on Saul's eyes fell off, restoring his sight. Afterward, Saul got up and was baptized.[143] As was the case with Philip's baptizands, there was no waiting period, no time of instruction or preparation for Saul. It was the work of the Holy Spirit.

Saul, who was later renamed Paul, is credited with writing much of Christian scripture. Raymond Brown writes in his classic work *An Introduction to the New Testament*: "Next to Jesus, Paul has been the most influential figure in the history of Christianity. Although all the NT writers are working out the implications of Jesus for particular communities of believers, Paul in his numerous letters does this on the widest scale of all. That range, plus the depth of his thought and the passion of his involvement, have meant that since his letters became a part of the NT, no Christian has been unaffected by what he has written."[144] It is a fair pairing and assessment. Saul's conversion experience is also a timely metaphor for the North American church, which could use a fresh pair of eyes.

Walter Brueggemann writes in *A Way Other Than Our Own*: "Jesus reached beyond his people, beyond his perceived mandate, beyond his tradition, extending himself to the 'other.' ... All of us to some extent, hold the line against 'the other.' All of us, to some extent, know that our faith calls us out beyond that."[145] Saul, who was once a nationalist Jew and would go on to found multiethnic communities of faith, called into question our exclusive Christology and membership policies.[146] Saul's conversion raised questions about our understanding of salvation, sanctification, and justification—all of which he is known for, since Saul heard Jesus' voice before he gave his life as a disciple.

When Saul was going in the opposite direction, he met Jesus. Does the church's context determine who its members are and who will hear the gospel message? William Willimon tells us in *Why Jesus?* that "Jesus got into all manner of trouble because of whom he saved. Jesus saved people who nobody thought could be saved or even wanted to be saved."[147] Following Jesus' example, Saul was called to share the faith with the Gentiles, which represented non-Jews or foreigners.

Saul's conversion experience was a group project, and Ananias was assigned to be a part of it. William Willimon explains in *The Intrusive Word: Preaching to the Unbaptized* that "Evangelism is a church... process." Nobody gets converted to Christianity in a vacuum. Every true conversion takes place in a socio-historical context. And it takes time. ... evangelism changes not only the convert but also the context. ... While I am in favor of changing the world, right now I would most like to change the church."[148] Willimon says that the church needs conversion, its own "Damascus Road" experience—and I agree with him.

James Baldwin says rightly in a *New York Times* article published in 1969, "I will flatly say that the bulk of this country's white population impresses me and has so impressed me for a very long time, as being beyond any conceivable hope of moral rehabilitation. They have been white, if I may so put it, too long."[149] *White Too Long* is the title of Robert P. Jones' book, and complements Baldwin's reasoning that whites are beyond redemption:

> This book puts forward a simple proposition: it is time—indeed well beyond time—for white Christians in the United States to reckon with the racism of our past and the willful amnesia of our present. Underneath the glossy, self-congratulatory histories that white Christian churches have written about themselves is a thinly veiled, deeply troubling reality. White Christian churches have not just been complacent; they have not only been complicit; rather, as the dominant cultural power in America, they have been responsible for constructing and sustaining a project to protect white supremacy and resist black equality. This project has framed the entire American story.[150]

Jones is calling for a "come to Jesus meeting," realizing that it is well past time to challenge and to change this identity.

Socially-colored white Christians will also need to address the coloring in of the face of God as white, in the person of Jesus, racializing the Trinity and in turn, divinizing whiteness and socially-colored white people who, not surprisingly, often struggle with a white savior (industrial) complex or syndrome.[151] In their book *The Color of Christ: The Son of God and the Saga of Race in America*, Edward J. Blum and Paul Harvey write,

> The white American Jesus first rose to power and prominence in the early nineteenth century. This was an era of the expansion of slavery and the often fraudulent and violent grabbing of Native American lands. It was also a moment of nation building and defining. Whiteness became a crucial symbol of national identity and citizenship. A new band of Protestants tried to win the young nation for Jesus by mass-producing and mass-distributing him. His racial affiliation, however, was soon embroiled in controversy. ... The Civil War, emancipation, and radical Reconstruction fractured white

national unity and cut the direct ties between whiteness and citizenship. This opened the door for challenges to the association of Jesus with whiteness.[152]

Racializing Jesus' gospel would segregate everything with two churches, two heavens and two hells, two Gods, two Saviors[153] and two devils, which came in black or white.

It would inspire the African American spirituals, which assisted in deconstructing American slavery. In *The Spiritual and the Blues*, James Cone writes, "It is not likely that songs so concretely related to the oppression of slavery would revert to abstraction or metaphor when speaking of freedom. … Both the African heritage and the slave experience guaranteed that the black spirituals would not be imprisoned by white definitions of God's liberating work." Both decoding and coding their experience, the ancestors' songs ensured that they all got the message.

It also prompted theological inquiry around divine and "religious racism," wherein "God's favor or disfavor is correlated with the racial or ethnic identity of the group in question" among other things.[154] It would inspire William R. Jones to ask, "Is God a white racist?" and the creation of liberation theology in response to oppressive spiritual and social conditions, separating the God of the oppressed from the God of the oppressor.[155] The Jesus of Nazareth and the Jesus of America were so far removed that the liberating nature of his message needed to be restated because the sociopolitical construct of race changed who his good news was for, namely socially-colored white people only.

Race not only changed the meaning and the message but also the point of Jesus' gospel, which has been supplanted by the good news of skin and its social coloring. Buchner Payne, an American clergyman, publisher, and racist pamphleteer of the nineteenth century, made this plain, saying,

Now as Adam was white, Abraham was white and our Savior white, did he enter heaven when he arose from the dead as a white man or a negro? If as a white man, then the negro is left out; if as a negro then the white man is left out. As Adam was the Son of God and as God is light (white) and in Him is no darkness (black) at all, how could God then be the father of the negro, as like begets like? And if God could not be the father of the blacks because He is white, how could our Savior, "being the express image of God's person," as asserted by St. Paul carry such a damned color into heaven, where all are white, much less to the throne?[156]

For Payne and many other Christians, it all points back to whiteness and socially-colored white people. Everything, including the plan of God, is about race.

But race wasn't a part of God's plan. Dying to the old self, baptizands were to identify as members of Christ's body. Paul wrote to the community of believers at Corinth: "For in the one Spirit we were all baptized into one body—Jews or Greeks, slaves or free—and we were all made to drink of one Spirit."[157] For Christians, these distinctions were to make no difference.

While not mentioned in the Bible, this rule can also apply to the sociopolitical construct of race as it seeks to position European Americans, those socially-colored white, over and above persons who are not members of this in-group. Jesus modeled it, and we even have a creed for it. What Paul shared with the communities of faith at Galatia and Colossae are the instructions for admission and the way in which these citizens of God's "kindom" will be identified once they rise from the water of baptism. Getting into a body of living water for this purpose carried significant meaning. Associated with the death, burial, and resurrection of Jesus, this was especially the case during Easter. Sandra M. Schneiders writes in "Scripture and Spirituality,"

> The celebration of baptism in connection with the solemnity of the resurrection (Easter) was an initiation of the Christian mystery of Christ in his passion, death, and resurrection understood against the background of creation, the fall, the flood, the promise to the ancestors, the exodus, the covenant, the exile, and the return, all understood as types of the salvation finally effected in Christ and now communicated to the members of the believing community.[158]

Baptism summed up everything. In and through baptism, the Christian story made sense.

The baptismal waters were full of meaning. When a baptizand stepped in, they could draw upon all these stories. Before Genesis 9:18-29, renamed "the curse of Ham," was conveniently used to justify the economic exploitation, inhumane treatment, and lifelong enslavement of Africans in America as "ordained by God" and a part of the natural order of things, baptism was used to determine one's status of slave or free in American society. The meaning and immediate implications of baptism were taken seriously. In Virginia's General Assembly in September 1667, an act was passed regarding baptism and exemption from enslavement. A problem had bubbled up:

> Whereas some doubts have risen whether children that are slaves by birth, and by the charity and piety of their owners made pertakers of the blessed sacrament of baptisme, should by virtue of their baptisme be made free. The assembly responded, "It is enacted and declared by this grand assembly, and by the authority thereof, that the conferring of baptisme doth not alter the condition of the person as to his bondage or ffreedome; that diverse masters, freed from this doubt, may more carefully endeavour the propagation of christianity by permitting children, though slaves, or those of greater growth if capable to be admitted to that sacrament.[159]

For Africans who were enslaved, this was no longer a path to freedom.

Christian colonizers knew the implications of baptismal water, that this act designated the baptizand as God's own, now identified with and through Jesus the Christ and as a member of his body. Accountable only for one's confession of faith and good as new due to baptismal regeneration,[160] St. Augustine of Hippo went so far as to say that baptism removed the stain of original sin.[161] European colonizers would mediate their relationship with the Divine and connection to their Creator. Baptism would be the dividing line.

A connection could be made between American slavery's depravity and the belief that enslaved African people had no soul since they had been re-created as property. In his autobiography, *With Head and Heart*, Howard Thurman tells a story of a little girl who thought she couldn't feel pain. He also provides the personal implications for such societal beliefs in *The Search for Common Ground*, writing:

> The body is a (person's) intimate dwelling place; it is (one's) domain as nothing else can ever be. It is coextensive with (oneself). If, for any reason whatsoever, a (person) is alienated in (one's) own body either by shame, outrage, or brutality, (one's) sense of community within (oneself) is rendered difficult, if not impossible. … It is for this reason that when (persons) wish to break the will, the inner entity of others, they resort to direct and violent cruelty upon their bodies. The aim here is to force a (person) to abdicate (their) body and thereby become an alien in (their) own house. This cuts (the person) off from the sustaining source of (their) own physical being; (the person) becomes disembodied and to that extent beingless.[162]

Baptismal identity and its freedoms were to be embodied, acted out, and supported by the community.

Calls for freedom were given voice throughout Christian scripture. Enslaved African Americans sang, "Go down, Moses, way down in Egypt's land." They created double meanings for speech that transcended the temporal reality of American slavery that was future-oriented and liberating, a means through which to understand their experience and to reason theologically with their Christian oppressors. They would also use baptism to make their case for manumission.

There's something about baptismal water. Why else would Jesus stand in line to be immersed in it? He came to John from Galilee for this purpose. Not wasting his pilgrimage, Jesus waved away the concerns of John, who was wasting his breath talking about his worthiness. This was not the time, and the Jordan River was not the place for such discussions.[163] Jesus offered a demonstration. It was his crucifixion practice. He reassured John, "Let it be so for now; for it is proper for us in this way to fulfill all righteousness."[164] The reversal of roles would later make sense.

The meanings would be drawn out as his disciples drew near his body. Of course, Jesus employed water as a sign of liberation from the former self and the old way of living. It harkened back to Hebrew Scripture and the story of the children of Israel's deliverance from the Egyptians. They "waded in the water," but it caused trouble for their enemies.[165]

Baptism is also not unlike the ritual washing known as *tvilah*, the Jewish practice of immersion in a body of water.[166] Everett Ferguson writes, however, that Christian baptism is not derived from bathing customs: "Much more likely is that the action was influenced by Jewish ritual washings, mediated and transformed by John the Baptist."[167] Perhaps this is why Peter took issue at least initially with the Gentiles in Acts 10. After the Holy Spirit fell upon them, he exclaimed, "Can anyone withhold the water for baptizing these people who have received the Holy Spirit just as we have?"[168] In Christian Scripture, new believers are instructed—as in the case of the Ethiopian treasurer—while others are baptized almost immediately.[169] Still, the water of baptism has been a source of contention because of the depth of its meaning.

The understanding of baptism was not without charges of heresy against groups whose practice was viewed as unorthodox. For example, in responding to the Gnostics, Irenaeus emphasized the Trinitarian formula and the inclusion of the Divine Community in support of the faith tradition handed down from the apostles. *Writing in Against Heresies*, he instructed: "First of all, [it] admonishes us to remember that we have received baptism for remission of sins in the name of God the Father, and in the name of Jesus Christ, the Son of God, who became incarnate and died and was raised, and in the Holy Spirit of God."[170] Other groups accused of heresy were the Marcionites and the Valentinians, whose beliefs we are made aware of through the response of their critics. The Marcionites differed in that they believed baptism required celibacy.[171] The Valentinians offered two baptisms, which Origen disagreed with based on Ephesians 4:5.[172] These responses provide insight into the convictions of early Christians.

In his treatise *On Baptism*, Tertullian responded to a member of the Cainite sect, whom he labeled "a female viper," having led some of the members astray, claiming there was no value to water baptism. Through his response, we get this ecclesiological gem: "little fishes" "are kept safe only by abiding in the water."[173] He adds insult to her teaching, writing, "That most monstrous woman, who had no right to teach even sound doctrine [1 Tim. 2:12], knew full well how to kill the little fishes by taking them away from the water."[174] The unnamed woman's denial of the efficacy of baptismal water was too much for him to bear so much, so that he praised the water in connection with creation.

Early church leaders also took the baptismal water seriously. They treated the water both literally and spiritually. While Origen did not address baptism singularly, he made an Old Testament connection to baptism in *Homilies on Exodus,* writing, "What the Jews supposed to be a crossing of the sea, Paul calls a baptism; what they supposed to be a cloud, Paul asserts is the Holy Spirit" (5.1).[175] St. Augustine's sermons, teachings, timeline, and commitment for the baptizand before baptism remind us that the decision was weighed heavily. John Chrysostom also thought it important for the baptizand or "newly illumined," as he referred to them, to understand the differences between Christ's baptism and Christian baptism, as the former had no need of redemption for the forgiveness of sins. He made this distinction in his sermon "On the Baptism of Christ."[176]

In the fourth century, there was still infighting. This time, it involved Athanasius, the bishop of Alexandria, who used baptism to make his argument against the Arians regarding the Godhead. Writing in *Discourses Against the Arians,* he said, "When baptism is given, whom the Father baptizes, him the Son baptizes; and whom the Son baptizes, he is consecrated in the Holy Spirit. ... Where the Father is or is named, there clearly is the Son also. Is the Father named in baptism? Then must the Son be named with him."[177]

For Athanasius, the baptizand is passed around to the members of the Trinity for baptism, which he holds in high regard and hopes that no one would reject "the grace of the font."[178] Baptism then is not only central to the practice of faith but also to one's understanding of the Trinity. Again and again, baptism is used to explain the Christian faith and as a means by which to examine a person's worthiness for the practice of the religion.

A friend of Athanasius, Serapion, wrote a collection of prayers, *The Prayer Book of Serapion*. Of the thirty prayers, seven are about baptism— namely, its sanctification, mystery, regeneration, and the worthiness of the baptizand. The Canons of Hippolytus, written in Arabic and later translated, includes a record of forty days of catechesis. In canon nine of thirty-eight, there is even a stipulation for the catechumen who is enslaved, but whose master does not want him to be baptized, to be given the assurance that "even if he dies without having received the gift, he is not excluded from the flock."[179] The rules and regulations for baptism are lengthy and given considerable treatment, including the type of water to be used in the ritual.

Didymus considered all kinds of water as viable options. Baptism could be performed in any body of water, including the sea. He pointed to Genesis 1:2 and Psalm 29:23 for justification.[180]

During the course of the "baptismal movements," the water was considered throughout the centuries and conditions were strained through it like sickbed baptism, the baptism of the dead, and on behalf of the deceased. Whether to immerse or asperse (sprinkle), the amount of water necessary for regeneration was examined critically. The age of the baptizand, whether an infant[181] or adult, made theologies distinct. The administrator of baptism, whether self-immersion or in community with the support of a pastor or priest, was also weighed heavily. There were debates about the number of times a person needed to be baptized, whether once or three, and if re-baptism was necessary.

The baptismal event, namely of Jesus, was so deeply meaningful that it was etched in stone in places such as the Catacomb of San Callisto in the third century repeatedly. Great lengths were taken to communicate the theological significance of baptism, evidenced by the ornate decoration of smaller baptismal fonts for infants and larger baptisteries for adults. Early versions were freestanding buildings, and fonts and often came in meaningful shapes. All of this is evidence of the intentional ways in which the understanding of baptism was shaped.

More than a ritual, this mystical reenactment of the death, burial, and resurrection of Jesus offers a lens through which Christian believers can see themselves clearly. There is something about the water, proven in that Jesus is in on it. Entry point and exit strategy, Jesus says to Nicodemus, "Very truly, I tell you, no one can enter the kingdom of God without being born of water and Spirit."[182] In baptism, we are coming and going, dying and reemerging as "a new creation," no longer regarded "from a human point of view."[183] Half in and half out of the water, the members of the church in North America have yet to see themselves through a baptismal identity.

Christian believers need only to look to Paul's letter to the communities at Galatia and Colossae. While Paul is known for the inclusion of the Gentiles into the Christian community, it is important to state unequivocally that his letters have been used to justify systems of oppression, hegemony, patriarchy, bigotry, misogyny, and othering. Elisabeth Schussler Fiorenza writes in *Paul and Politics: Ekklesia, Israel, Imperium, Interpretation*:

> One of the negative legacies of Pauline discourse is its inscribed politics of "othering." Such a politics and rhetorics of othering establishes identity by declaring the difference of the other as the same or by vilifying and idealizing difference as otherness. It justifies relationships of ruling by obfuscating structures of domination and subordination as "naturalized" differences. Hence, this politics of othering can be changed only when it is understood not as a universal transcultural binary structure or given revelation but as a historical political practice.[184]

Simply put, Christians do it because this is the way that it has always been done. They do not know how to experience themselves or each other differently and as a member of Christ's body despite being baptized in Jesus' name and receiving a baptismal identity.

But Paul does something worth noting in his letters to the communities of Corinth and Colossae. It's not a fluke or a hope unfounded for the early church members. Paul talks about the work and witness of baptism repeatedly. To the church at Corinth, Christian believers are encouraged to take it all in, "all made to drink of one spirit," to drink from the same cup Jesus offered his disciples.[185] To the believers at Colossae, Paul speaks to exchanging a temporal, bodily identity for a transcendent one, saying, "In him also you were circumcised with a spiritual circumcision, by putting off the body of the flesh in the circumcision of Christ; when you were buried with him in baptism, you were also raised with him through faith in the power of God, who raised him from the dead."[186]

Time and time again, Paul talks about the Christian community as a body of believers.[187] It is fitting, as Christians are identified with Christ's body. Likewise, Jesus asked, "Can you drink the cup I must drink, or be baptized with the baptism with which I must be baptized?"[188] To follow Christ is to die to self.[189] His disciples enter what some have referred to as a "watery grave."

Galatians 3:27-28 and Colossians 3:10-11 specifically provide the spiritual framework for this recreation narrative and the raceless gospel, which is a liberating message that transcends the carnal categories of race. Forgotten before it was ever put into practice, it is considered by some scholars to be the church's first creed. In Galatians 3, it is inserted and seemingly appears out of place. Paul begins the chapter questioning the mental agility and/or stability of the Galatians. They have forgotten the work of Christ's cross: that in, by, and through faith in Jesus there is no more work to be done. Abraham is given as an example of believing by faith and afterwards, Paul teaches them on the purpose of the law. There is nothing that their bodies need to do to earn this relationship with God; they need only to believe.

Then Paul writes, "As many of you as were baptized into Christ have clothed yourselves with Christ. There is no longer Jew or Greek, there is no longer slave or free, there is no longer male and female; for all of you are one in Christ Jesus."[190] These are not the words of Paul; he merely copied them.[191] Still, they are about life after baptism, the work of the water and the witness of new birth.

Once baptized, the Christian believer's life is fully submerged and fully surrendered to Jesus—at least in theory. Stephen J. Patterson's seminal work *The Forgotten Creed: Christianity's Original Struggle Against Bigotry, Slavery, & Sexism* tells another story. Patterson concludes that "this creed has played virtually no role. How could it? The church became a citadel of patriarchy and enforced this regime wherever it spread. It also endorsed and encouraged the taking of slaves from the people it colonized. And within a hundred years of its writing, 'no Jew or Greek' simply became 'no Jews,' as the church separated from, then rebelled against its Jewish patrimony, eventually attempting patricide."[192]

There is no dividing line, no "us versus them," no groups, no clans, no tribes. Patterson makes a fine point, writing, "These are not distinctions of religion and culture, but of power and privilege."[193] Consequently, Christians are identified solely with the body of Christ, who "emptied himself."[194]

It is also a biblical response to the marginalization of people groups, the patriarchal domination of women, and the economic exploitation of persons who are enslaved. It is a counter to the ancient cliché: "I thank God every day that I was born a native, not a foreigner; free and not a slave; a man and not a woman."[195] Patterson translates the first words of the creed, "For you are all children of God through faith in Christ Jesus,"[196] which—it bears repeating—calls into question the ongoing sibling rivalries.

Paul says it again to the believers at Colossae. In Colossians 3, he explains the new life of the believer and the behavior that is expected. Raised with Christ, he has high expectations for Jesus' followers. Baptized with Jesus, carnal desires have been executed, "put to death."[197] Consequently, it is one's former life and considered "the old self."

But a change, or regeneration, comes through baptism. Paul writes, "In that renewal, there is no longer Greek or Jew, circumcised or uncircumcised, barbarian, Scythian, slave and free; but Christ is all and in all!"[198] Again, Paul addresses these false binaries, and this time includes circumcision, which had been a sticking point for the church at Jerusalem in Acts 11. It is settled through Peter's vision and the words of Jesus he remembered: "And I remembered the word of the Lord, how he said, 'John baptized with water, but you will be baptized with the Holy Spirit.'"[199] His report to the church members settled it; the Gentiles were not to be excluded. Baptism was a means of reforming the early church.

There is an expression that goes like this: "They called me everything but a child of God." In baptism, the believer is exactly that—able to claim God as next of kin. How then did some Christians think that race would be able to deny this divine parentage? The hymnist sang, "Take me to the water to be baptized." The answer is there.

Christians must "wade in the water" and talk about why baptismal identity has never caused trouble for race or its segregating identities. The gospel was supposed to make waves. Jesus' followers must discuss how the church in North America conspired with capitalism to drown out its implications during American slavery and how baptism's meaning was watered down to protect the master and slave classes and the competing ways of human being and belonging. Stanley J. Grenz writes in *Theology for the Community of God*,

> The act of repentance and faith constitutes a grand reorientation of our community of participation. We lay aside whatever old allegiances formerly demanded our loyalty and to turn to the God revealed in Jesus Christ. In conversion, we forsake the loyalties of our former community of participation and accept as our own the allegiance to Christ embodied by his community. We disassociate ourselves from the faith confession of all other communities; with the community of Christ, we confess faith in Jesus as Lord.[200]

Race has created another gospel, another community with whiteness as the competing identity for lordship.

Thus, the raceless gospel doubles as a teaching instrument and an emerging ecclesiology that is egalitarian, nonbinary, nondualistic.[201] It is proclaimed in response to an undivided "kin-dom" that is coming, which doesn't view race as a determinant for membership and belonging. Paul's words to the believers at Galatia and Colossae are critical to our confession of faith. The raceless gospel invites us to re-read scripture as an expression of "faith seeking understanding"—without the lens of race.

The Bible does not talk about race. But Paul's words to the Corinthian believers put the seventeenth-century invention in its place. Paul writes what should be obvious to all readers: "Not all flesh is alike, but there is one flesh for human beings, another for animals, another for birds, and another for fish."[202] His words blatantly contradict the theory of race created by European Enlightenment thinkers.

In his 1776 volume *On the Natural Varieties of Mankind,* Johann Friedrich Blumenbach, who coined the word Caucasian to describe the "white race," said there were five races: Caucasian, Mongoloid, Ethiopian, American, and Malay. Swedish botanist-taxonomist-zoologist Carolus Linnaeus created binomial nomenclature and said human beings came in four varieties: Homo Europaeus, Homo Asiaticus, Homo Afer, and Homo Americanus. Georges Cuvier and John Hunter both counted three. Paul Topinard had nineteen and placed them under three headings. Edmund Burke managed to find sixty-three races.[203] Presently, we settle on five—six, if you're counting—not rooted in country of origin but color: beige (mixed race), black, brown, red, yellow, and white. Naturalist George Louis Leclerc Buffon argued that "white" was "normative and the real and natural color of man." The raceless gospel declares there is no longer beige or black, brown or red, white or yellow people: we are all children of God and members of Christ's body.

Race has not been fully submerged in the waters of baptism by the North American church, but the handwriting is on the wall with books such as *The Baptism of Early Virginia: How Christianity Created Race* (Rebecca Anne Goetz), *After Whiteness: An Education in Belonging* (Willie James Jennings), and *White Theology: Outing Supremacy in Modernity* (James W. Perkinson). Perkinson even argues for a "post-white vocation," the transfiguration of power and the initiation of baptism because "white supremacy is one of the preeminent 'principalities and powers' of our time."[204] Increasingly, racialized identities are being viewed as arbitrary and there is a desire for a fuller, freer expression of human identity. It is found in the language of baptism and the confession of the baptizand who has taken on a baptismal identity. The raceless gospel addresses not only racism but also its source—

race. It is in line with the civil rights leaders, inspired by the African American religious experience, who made their faith public by challenging America's social order, evidenced then and now by segregation. The raceless gospel is a continuation of that proclamation of "somebodiness" and the challenge their work and witness put forth.

The raceless gospel is rooted in a transcendent expression of human being and belonging as God's children and as seen through the lens of Galatians 3:27-28 and expanded upon in Colossians 3:10-11. It is the embodiment of the first creed. These dyads, false binaries, and oppositional ways of being and belonging are submerged in the water of baptism. The baptismal creed goes against whom the society supported and endorsed as worthy of belonging.

Summarily, it is important for persons who are seeking fullness in Christ to not solely talk about what race has done to us but what race is doing *through* our bodies. If Christians are to believe and behave as the body of Christ, then a complete and thorough examination of the impact of its racialization and subsequent segregation is imperative. Christian believers must move the conversation inward, as baptism has an internal orientation. The raceless gospel takes the church to the water and uses the baptistry as a reflection pool. Because there's something about the water that changes how Christians see things and if it doesn't, then I would test it.

CHAPTER 3

Testing the Waters

Take me to the water,
Take me to the water,
Take me to the water,
To be baptized

Can you believe it? From misfits to micromanagers of a religious experience, from crucifixion spectators to curators of the pastor's movements, from house churches to multimillion-dollar buildings, from donkeys to private jets, from tuna fish sandwiches to star-studded events, the North American church has come a long way from Calvary.

Can you believe it? The North American church's leader, Jesus, rose from the grave. Yet the institution remains in a compromising position, its tongue tied to the American government and tied down by its political allegiances. The resurrected body of Christ split in two as if the Divine can be split into Democrat and Republican sides, as if God has only two sides and we have seen both. The glory of God revealed in those we vote for, we pull the lever and live to see the work of our hands. It's heresy. God is not a politician and does not need to lie.

Can you believe that the North American church would reduce the Word made flesh to the U.S. Constitution, the mysterious ways of God to a voting bloc, and the will of God to a fifty-year political strategy? We've got God all figured out, all worked out, all the divine Persons working for our side of the equation. Then, we wonder why nothing balances out. The Trinity plus you versus me equals systemic inequality and inequity with a pseudo-theological backing.

The power of God is reserved solely for America's protection and the annihilation of its enemies, to ensure that the country accumulates the most territory and wealth but not before enacting genocidal violence to ensure that its victims do not live to tell the story. Can you believe it? Can you believe that the North American church would attempt to confine the God who created worlds and galaxies to America's shores and suggest that God's vested interest lies with these fifty states and those islands it holds hostage and no more?

Painted into a corner of the world as a socially-colored white man, which props up the sociopolitical construct of race, white supremacy, and the patriarchy... How convenient! But none of these pop up in descriptions or depictions of God in the Hebrew or Christian Scriptures. So don't believe it.

Do we really believe that the movements of God are in lockstep with America's own? With Caesar as the head, we enlist God in the fight for the American right to go anywhere and take everything. But I'm scratching my head because this is not what Jesus said. I'm tilting my head because this is not what Jesus did. I'm shaking my head because this is not what Jesus died for.

I'm banging my head against a brick wall because this is not what Jesus was building on when he said, "Upon this rock, I will build my church."[205] This is not to be confused with the church as enterprise, as franchise—one church in three locations, tax-exempt, and doing business as usual. This is unusual, given Jesus' example. What am I witnessing?

Because God's prophets are now fortunetellers who only see good things, crying, "Blessing, blessing" while we live under the curse of capitalism. The early church used to go from house to house. Now we meet for an hour twice a week.[206] The fullness of Christ wrongly equated with full pews, now reduced to near-empty church buildings... Can you believe it?

The North American church exchanged its prophetic voice for power plays, to be in pictures with this piece of work in progress, on the brink of self-destruction, attacking itself again—first the Civil War and now an insurrection. "This is America."[207] But activist-clergyman Allan Boesak stated, "When I say, 'Jesus,' I say, 'Justice' and when I say, 'Justice,' I say, 'Jesus.'" His words lead me to believe that if Jesus is in the neighborhood, then so is justice. So where is this justice-minded and always-up-to-earthly-good, Jesus? I didn't see him at a single business or committee meeting, calling for a vote on our cultural way of following him. I didn't see him down in the fellowship hall, saying, "If you baked a cake for the pastor, then you have fed me."

The head of the church is not a figurehead, a bobblehead Jesus, "Jesus Christ Superstar," the Jesus you claim looks just like you, the Jesus you frame and hang in your sanctuaries and homes. Where is the servant Jesus—God in the flesh and with us, on the move and in our midst, without a home, without a life insurance policy or retirement plan? Where is this Jesus, in whom the fullness of the Divine dwells bodily, which is not to be confused with the Jesus product stocked on store shelves? He's not in aisle two, and a stock clerk can't reach up to pull him down for you.

Forget what you've heard. Because this Jesus goes over our heads. Still, the North American church preaches "another gospel"[208]—a prosperity gospel, a partisan gospel, a pigmented gospel. But baptism cuts us off from the flesh, its alliances and allegiances, the self-gratification of power and prestige. The raceless gospel reminds us to feel the waves that covered our bodies and then our faces; to keep in mind the depth of our commitment to Christ and his body, which makes us alive and free from the captivity of this flesh.

Raised from the dead, we praise this new body that believes there is a way to dwell with Christ that puts off the world and its ways, that believes we can live freely and grow out of this world in preparation for the next, for an undivided "kin-dom"[209] that is on its way. It's in the water. May we take hard steps until we are in too deep; until labels float to the top; until we come clean about who we really are; until all other competing, misleading, and deceiving voices are drowned out; until we only hear the voice of Jesus calling; until we are in over our heads.

How can the raceless gospel expressed through a baptismal pedagogy act as a catalyst for desegregating sacred space? Can a baptismal pedagogy informed by the raceless gospel, as depicted and determined by Galatians 3:27-28 and Colossians 3:9-11, make both an ecclesiological and ontological difference? If we take the North American church to the waters of baptism, does baptismal regeneration[210] lead Christian believers to divest of the color-coded categories assigned to them in America based on the sociopolitical construct of race? Does the act of immersive baptism, one's subsequent identification as a "baptized believer" and embodiment of a baptismal identity then call into question a racialized body and subsequently the racialized body of Christ, which is the North American church?[211] Further, can a deeper understanding of baptism challenge the church's current practice of Sunday morning segregation?

How did this Jewish Jesus get in the middle of this? Christians cannot deny Jesus' cultural heritage as a Jew "according to the flesh"[212] or his relationship to Judaism, as it is historically accurate and for their faith, necessary for the fulfillment of the Messianic prophecies in Hebrew scriptures.[213] Thus, one must wonder why Jesus has been racialized, re-created as blonde-haired and blue-eyed,[214] and fitted to a culturally assimilated image of an American Jesus. "American Christians no longer come together around theology or a book. Yet they are united in their love of Jesus," writes Stephen Prothero in *American Jesus: How the Son of God Became a National Icon*.[215] Still, Christians disagree on his image, an image that has no bearing in scripture, does not serve a single creedal confession, and is not the basis for which to receive him. Jesus said, "Let anyone with ears listen!"[216]

The Christian believer's need for Jesus' physical features to reflect one's own is in response to white supremacy. Apart from the sociopolitical construct of race, there is no biblical basis, spiritual discipline, or religious justification for re-creating Jesus in our own image and consequently, to racialize his gospel. Recontextualizing his message to suit the aims of colonialism, white supremacy, and Christian nationalism—or as a response to them— changes the direction and aim of the gospel, which was never about race. This does not suggest that Jesus is not on the side of the oppressed or that liberation theology is unnecessary. But centering race and therein salvation in and through *our* flesh and whiteness, namely, and not *his* changes the salvific message entirely. Instead of disrupting the caste system by reordering the hierarchy with the response to white power being black power or red power,[217] there is a need for an ecclesiology that destabilizes whiteness by deconstructing race vis-à-vis decentering whiteness and then dismantling it.

The raceless gospel questions "by what authority"[218] does race determine what Christians see in Jesus and what they are looking for in a savior. Why did they follow him to the water to be baptized if the act does not address "the slander of invisibility,"[219] as is the case for African Americans? Do they need Jesus to look like "us" and not "them" to follow in his footsteps? Do North American Christians view baptism as a cleansing, wherein we wash our hands of "those people" and give thanks that we are not them? Or is it a drowning, resulting in the death of the divided self and all its prejudices never to be seen or heard from again? New birth suggests the latter.

The raceless gospel then calls into question our practice of discipleship. Because if race determines whether we can see Jesus as our savior and defines fellowship in his name, then we are not gathering as his body. Returning to our baptism and the baptismal waters would allow us to look at Jesus again or perhaps even for the first time. N.T. Wright says in *Following Jesus: Biblical Reflections on Discipleship,*

> The longer you look at Jesus, the more you will want to serve him in his world. That is, of course, if it's the real Jesus you're looking at. Plenty of people in the church and outside it have made up a 'Jesus' for themselves and have found that this invented character makes few real demands on them. He makes them feel happy from time to time but doesn't challenge them, doesn't suggest that they get up and do something about the plight of the world. Which is, of course, what the real Jesus had an uncomfortable habit of doing.[220]

We need only look at the life of Paul as an example of conversion, a murderer turned missionary to the Gentiles, who was viewed as a symbol of a bridge too far because of his calling to include them.

The raceless gospel as a baptismal pedagogy elevates the importance of the Christian believer's inward orientation and spiritual life. It facilitates an encounter with the self, explained in striking language by Howard Thurman in *The Inward Journey*:

> ... there comes a deep necessity which leads you finally into the closet with yourself. It is here that you raise the real questions about yourself. The leading one is, What is it, after all, that I amount to, ultimately? Such a question cuts through all that is superficial and trivial in life to the very nerve center of yourself. And this is a religious question because it deals with the total meaning of life at its heart. At such a moment, ... you must discover for yourself what is the *true* basis of your self-respect. This is found only in relation to God whose Presence makes itself known in the most lucid moments of self-awareness. For all of us are (God's) children and the most crucial clue to a knowledge of (God) is to be found in the most honest and most total knowledge of the self.[221]

Consequently, the questions that race asks of us, which are based solely on physicality, do not address the real meaning of the self as "a living soul"[222] and one's Christian identity but ensures a superficial existence wherein everyone remains a stranger—even to oneself.

Questions such as "What does it mean to be black and Christian?"[223] are evidence of the ontological challenges that race creates within the Christian faith and that permeate theological dialogue. Thus, there remains a pressing need for baptismal water and new words that call us to an unclaimed and unnamed space within, which is unable to be defined by the economic, political, and social forces of our day. But it requires deep listening for what Howard Thurman calls "the sound of the genuine." He told a group of graduates at Spelman College in May of 1980:

> There is something in every one of you that waits, listens for the genuine in yourself—and if you cannot hear it, you will never find whatever it is for which you are searching and if you hear it and then do not follow it, it was better that you had never been born. You are the only you that has ever lived; your idiom is the only idiom of its kind in all the existences, and if you cannot hear the sound of the genuine in you, you will all of your life spend your days on the ends of strings that somebody else pulls.[224]

There is an internal calling that is genuine and an external calling from the American empire that is entirely and purposefully misleading to ensure command, control, and a life lived in comparison to others—which keeps the capitalist machinery going with race, ensuring the American mind-wheels turning in service to it.

Race muddies the baptismal waters and contributes to the classic narrative of North America as the promised land, based on democratic principles—which remain largely aspirational—the kingdom of God, and "a city on a hill." North America as the kingdom of God is the traditional interpretation of American religion. It treats Jesus as an immigrant, forced to assimilate to be accepted in America. It also forces a narrative of exclusion/inclusion based on the prescriptions of whiteness, which is also a social construction.

That may be good news for us, but not for him. David E. Fitch wrote in *The Church of Us vs. Them*, "it seems that dividing is in the DNA of Christendom."[225] But this was not the aim of his gospel. Paul wrote to the church at Ephesus: "For he is our peace; in his flesh he has made both into one and has broken down the dividing wall, that is, the hostility between us, abolishing the law with its commandments and ordinances, that he might create in himself one new humanity in place of the two, thus making peace, and might reconcile both to God in one body through the cross, thus putting to death that hostility through it."[226]

Antagonism now dead and born again, "a new creation,"[227] Jesus' death and resurrection, having been "raised for them,"[228] provides a new life for his followers. This changes the believer's perspective, regarding "no one from a human point of view."[229] Still, church historian George R. Knight said, "racial prejudice, like other sins, is not totally eradicated in most Christians at conversion. Nor are the racial tensions embodied in a culture easy for the churches existing in that culture to overcome."[230] In North America, even the body of Christ is then forced to identify with race and its categories, which challenges the power of Jesus' death and resurrection, the power made evident in baptism. If race cannot be taken to the water, then there is no "kin-dom" beyond caste.[231]

The sociopolitical construct of race wrongly dictates our understanding of conformity to Christ's image as a physical image and not to his resurrected body, which would be understandable, a moral conformity that is sanctification or a sacrificial conformity, which would explain our suffering.[232] Instead, it demands a certain physical appearance rather than act as a determinant for a familial bond "within a large family"[233] and a vocational emphasis in support of "his purpose."[234] Being conformed to Christ's image requires a re-creation not of our physical bodies but through the Word[235] we embody, and should not suffer simplistic reductions explained as being made "like Christ" but not spelled out explicitly.

As members of Christ's body, we are not required to assimilate to the domineering culture in support of the political narratives of North America or to change our physical appearance to blend in with the majoritized, or socially-colored white people. That is also the work of colonization. Ronald Rolheiser defines what the body of Christ means in no uncertain terms in *The Holy Longing*, where he wrote: "We are the Body of Christ. This is not an exaggeration, nor a metaphor. To say that the body of believers is the Body of Christ is not saying something that scripture does not. Scripture, and Paul in particular, never tells us that the body of believers *replaces* Christ's body, nor *represents* Christ's body, nor even that it is Christ's *mystical* body. It says simply: 'We are Christ's body.'"[236] Consequently, Christianity is a body language. For it to be heard, it must be seen and made evident by the members of Christ's body, his church.

As a former pastor and as is true for most if not all Christians, I view Bible study as essential to understanding and practicing the Christian faith. Christian education not only informs the believer of its tenets and traditions but also aids in the disciple's spiritual formation. Bible study is a principal service of the church, which is viewed as a place where people go to learn (more) about Jesus. To be clear, "the Bible's concern is not *if* we shall believe but *what* we shall believe."[237] My concern is what Christians believe about race.

It is also learning done in community with other believers. "Community is essential to epistemology," writes Stanely J. Grenz in *Theology for the Community of God*.[238] Community also assists with the formation of identity and, in this case, one's identity as a Christian believer. It is here that the convert learns that a follower of Jesus is a member of his body, and likewise, a member of one another.[239] It is where persons come to know Jesus, who is "not only currently active, but the 'kinship group' of which he is the common and defining 'ancestor' is here and now open to his agency, which is 'appropriated' to its human members, in the sense that what they do and say in the name or persona of Jesus counts as done and said by Jesus," writes Rowan Williams in *Christ: The Heart of Creation*.[240]

Since the North American church is a traditionally segregated space, this makes one's awareness of membership and belonging to Christ's raceless body difficult but not impossible—though most Americans are bred with the awareness of being viewed through a racialized lens.[241] Proof of one's Christian identity is largely thought to be expressed through being marked present in a building versus being joined as members of Christ's body. Thus, religious conditioning wherein one joins a church, becomes a member of a particular building, and learns their responsibilities as to how to maintain it is not to be confused with spiritual conversion. Regeneration should not be reduced to a change in physical location but in one's understanding of belonging.

This does not negate the need to gather or dismiss the historic and present need for African Americans to "claim a collective cultural identity as a way of strengthening their campaign to survive and live out their destiny of full humanity."[242] Instead, the raceless gospel for a baptismal pedagogy that leads to a desegregated church seeks to undermine the credibility of race and more specifically white supremacy by addressing its pseudoscientific foundation and linking the history of violence that comes with a belief in it. The raceless gospel would then reposition us in our deep sense of "somebodiness" and invite the minoritized and marginalized to no longer defend their humanity since we're all God's children.

Galatians 3:27-28 and Colossians 3:9-11, among other scriptures, offer a theologically corrective lens to view both the individual member and the corporate body of Christ. Coupled with the member's own experience of believer's baptism, a Bible study gathering could (1) assist in questioning the colonialist's prejudice of "natural inferiority" among believers, (2) allow for the discussion of the suppressed history of withholding baptism from enslaved Africans, and (3) provide an emphasis on the immediate effects on one's understanding and sense of self since "Rev. Charles Martyn, of South Carolina, complained that some baptized slaves 'became lazy and proud, entertaining too high an opinion of themselves and neglecting their daily labour.'"[243] A baptismal pedagogy that addresses the false narrative of race that has been intertwined with the Christian faith is grossly needed.

While the letters to the faith communities at Galatia and Colossae are the basis for the raceless gospel, "the politics of othering and vilification permeates the discourses of Paul himself."[244] Elizabeth Schussler Fiorenza writes in an essay titled "Paul and the Politics of Interpretation:" "Its relentless othering engenders the strategies of marginalization by contemporary exegetical and theological scholarship. Not just religious studies but all modern theories of political and moral life are shot through with the politics of othering, that is, with ideologies of sexism, colonialism, and racism, the systems and discourses of marginalization, vilification, and dehumanization."[245] Consequently, the use of both letters is not taken lightly.

The use of Paul's writings to the faith communities at Galatia and Colossae are a part of the tradition named by Delores S. Williams in *Sisters in the Wilderness* as the "liberation tradition of African American biblical appropriation." I have used Paul's writings and paradigm in four Bible studies to demonstrate the Christlike freedom of believers from hierarchical relationships and their power dynamics through one's baptismal identity.[246] Rather than remain in the social context that creates and maintains a racialized reality, the weekly lessons offer participants a glimpse into an undivided "kin-dom" that is coming. They can be offered with the understanding given by James Cone in *God of the Oppressed* that "To know God is to experience the acts of God in the concrete affairs and relationships of people, liberating the weak and the helpless from pain and humiliation."[247] The studies allow baptized believers to practically apply Christian scriptures to social conditions, namely a racialized existence, and to engage in deconstructing the social conditioning of race as a part of the spiritual discipline of self-mortification and the spiritual experience of regeneration.

If you need a Bible study, then consider "'Take me to the water': An examination of baptismal identity for a lukewarm Christianity." Following is a description that can be publicized in various ways: printed in the church bulletin and/or newsletter; posted on a bulletin board, a flatscreen in the sanctuary, your church's webpage and social media platforms; announced in church meetings and services; transmitted through a phone tree.

"'Take me to the water': An examination of baptismal identity for a lukewarm Christianity" seeks to explore the message, meaning, and models for living into a baptismal identity that challenges watered-down versions of Americanized Christianity. If you are unsure of where you would find this kind of curriculum, then keep reading. This chapter includes our first lesson and some practice at a conversation that the North American church should be having with itself.

LESSON I

1 Peter 3:18-22

Peter could not truly know Jesus apart from knowing himself in relation to Jesus. He did not know himself until Jesus showed him who he was. But in learning about himself, he also came to truly know Jesus. Deep knowing of God and deep knowing of self always develop interactively. The result is the authentic transformation of the self that is at the core of Christian spirituality.[248]

David G. Benner
The Gift of Being Yourself

There all are kinds of safe drinking water—unless you live in Flint, Michigan. I wonder, "What kind of water does baptism require?" Water that draws out what it means to follow Jesus and drowns out all the competing ways of human being? Water that strains and lessens birthing pains? What kind of water is this?

Holy water, river, stream, pond, baptistery filled with water... Three feet-, four feet-, five feet-, six feet-deep, bend-your-knees, tilt-your-head back, hold-your-nose, aid-in-your-own-burial kind of water... Warmed and freezing cold water... Dressed in white robes before we enter this water... Eulogy the same: "I baptize you in the name of the Father, the Son, and the Holy Spirit. Amen." Our entry into new life is a watery grave. We practice resurrection, Christ's resurrection.

Water that cleanses for the remission of sins, marks that one is born again and later is added as a condition of church membership... We are given a baptism certificate as if it is a finished work, as if we have done the salvific work ourselves. The right hand of fellowship does not seal the deal... Cleansing ritual and rite of passage, entry point and an exit strategy from the old self, old world, and its habits.

Baptism, *baptizo* for the Greeks, was adapted from the Jewish tradition of immersion in a ritual bath.[249] Jesus used water, infused water into our storied identity, turned water into wine, drove a herd of swine into the water for a man's deliverance. Water is natural and miraculous. As much as 60 percent of the adult human body is water, according to H.H. Mitchell in the *Journal of Biological Chemistry*. Water inside and out, watered within and without, baptism invites us to take on more water.

As baptized believers, we live watery lives. We walk with wet feet. We enter spaces dripping wet with proof of our death and new life with and in and through Jesus the Christ. Water drips from our lips and our hair and our fingertips onto floors padded, carpeted, wooden, earthen, scrubbed, polished, dusty, matted with gum and playdough, greasy, sticky, mixed with urine, milk, and coffee.

Stained… We get in the water, "the cleansing flood," after promises that we will be good, clean, saved, righteous. Fresh start, the water erases all that we were. Blank slate but not blank stares, we see as Christ sees now. We are his body.

We speak from submerged places of being. We go down in the deep and into dark spaces where human beings do not live. We go down into water with mammals—sharks, seahorses, whales, octopuses, and schools of fish. We go down deep where the Spirit hovers and calls us children of God.

Baptism is story-dependent. We are baptized because of the story of Jesus, but also because of our own story—our story that separates the good from bad people. Parting waters and drawing a line, baptism is part of our desire to become a good person, to be on the right side.

We want to be a part of the festivities, join in the shouting and singing. We want to become a member, receive the right hand of fellowship, join the flock, and have a shepherd, a pastor. We want to be saved from some past, present, or future bad person, place, or thing. We want to be saved from our past, present, and future self who was, is, and will be in bad places; who has done, is doing, and will do bad things. We just want to be called good, though God said it in the beginning.

Simon, Cephas, Peter, Rock… He is named first among the Twelve and as a member of the inner circle: Peter, James, and John. Talking loudly but saying nothing when Jesus was arrested and crucified, he denied Christ three times after professing his love for him.[250]

Jesus commissioned Peter: "feed my sheep."[251] Peter confessed that Jesus is the Messiah.[252] On this rock, this Peter, Jesus said he would build his church.[253] This Peter who walked side by side with Jesus, this Peter who made some mistakes and was not all good or all bad, wrote a letter to the scattered church as "an apostle of Jesus Christ."[254]

For Christ also suffered for sins once for all, the righteous for the unrighteous, in order to bring you to God. He was put to death in the flesh, but made alive in the spirit, in which he also went and made a proclamation to the spirits in prison, who in former times did not obey, when God waited patiently in the days of Noah, during the building of the ark, in which a few, that is, eight persons, were saved through water. And baptism, which this prefigured, now saves you—not as a removal of dirt from the body, but as an appeal to God for a good conscience, through the resurrection of Jesus

Christ, who has gone into heaven and is at the right hand of God, with angels, authorities, and powers made subject to him. (1 Pet. 3:18-22)

In this scripture, Peter testified to his relationship with Jesus and put it in writing. He said that baptism saves us, which is not to be confused with bath time. This is not a physical cleansing. This is a different kind of water. It doesn't clear up our skin, but it does clear our conscience.

Peter failed the loyalty test with three retakes. Still, Jesus trusted him with his church. With Paul, Peter would become a pillar of the early church. Later, he would die as a martyr under Nero's reign.

What does Peter's example say to you about goodness, righteousness, and the baptismal waters?

Questions

1. What is your relationship with water? What are your first memories: splashing, puddle-making, swimming, cleansing/washing?
2. How did you come to know what was goodness? How was your goodness defined and/or explained? Is there an image/word/phrase/story that comes to mind?
3. How does baptism inform your understanding of righteousness and/or right standing with God? What led you to the water?
4. Water as punishment is revisited in Peter's epistle through the story of Noah and how his family was saved from the water. What does this story say about the way God sorts human beings out using water?
5. Peter used the phrase, "saved through water." How has the water of baptism saved you?
6. Water baptism as witness bearing, we proclaim Jesus' resurrection. How has the church watered down the meaning of baptism and its daily life implications?
7. After our discussion of water, baptism, and our storied lives, what is floating to the top for you?

And just like that, you are reading scripture through a baptismal lens. If you're up to it, then let's do it again. I know that I said there would only be one lesson, but this is one that bears repeating. So, let's go deeper.

LESSON 2
Matthew 3:11

Baptism asserts that we meet and speak under an identity that challenges
and endangers all other identities.[255]

William H. Willimon
Peculiar Speech

In James Baldwin's play, *The Amen Corner*, Margaret Alexander, the pastor
of the church says, "… your mind ain't on the Lord. And if your mind ain't
stayed on Him, every hour of the day, Satan's going to cause you to fall."[256]
As a child, I would join with the congregation and sing, "Woke up this
morning with my mind / Stayed on Jesus / Woke up this morning with my
mind / Stayed on the Lord / Woke up this morning with my mind / Stayed
on Jesus / Hallelu-, Hallelu-, Hallelujah."

Some Christians came to faith the hard way, without a full understanding
of unmerited grace and the unconditional love of God. Some had yet to
learn that this is an inward journey and not a public appearance of holiness.
They had not been taught about the inwardness of religion that Howard
Thurman wrote about in *The Creative Encounter*: "There need not be only
one single rebirth, but again and again a (person) may be reborn until at last
there is nothing that remains between (a person) and God."[257] Again and
again, he says.

Like baptism's inner work, some baptized believers falsely believed that
our work consists mainly of right believing and behaving: no cursing, no
smoking, no drinking, no sex. Most often, they were too young to know
that faith goes so much deeper than this: that to go down in the water
doesn't mean that you come up with a list of do's and don'ts. This is not what
it means to be born again.

Matthew's gospel offers us two baptisms: John's baptism of water and
Jesus' baptism of Spirit and fire. This is good for a church that desperately
needs a "come to Jesus meeting," that needs to repent of its sins and be
delivered from its complicity with empire. Because we are not there yet. We
are looking at our baptism certificate, the words of Paul to the Galatians:
"There is no longer Jew or Greek, there is no longer slave or free, there is no
longer male and female for all of you are one in Christ Jesus"[258] and asking
Jesus, "Why aren't we *there* yet?"

Because we have been following Jesus but are still no closer to his vision
of a "kin-dom" coming. I'm in the backseat asking, "Why aren't we *there*

yet?" Were we supposed to turn there? Did we get off on the wrong exit? We carry big Bibles, so how did we miss it?

This looks so familiar. We have been here before, in this conflicted state. The church is always fighting, splitting hairs, splintering off, pointing fingers, and crossing people off their list. Across America and before the Covid-19 pandemic, we were standing in large but mostly empty church buildings, huddled in the vestibule discussing the latest opinion column about the "graying of the church." The direction we have been going in is getting us nowhere. So, I think this would be a good time to turn around and answer those children, the younger generations in the backseat, who are questioning the direction of the church. Because they realize why we aren't there yet. And they don't want to come along for the ride.

Nobody knew where Jesus was going or what he was talking about. He was rejected and misunderstood—no matter what he did or said.[259] All of this talk of suffering, death, and his resurrection... Not a single disciple, member of the worship committee or the crowd was following, and, in the end, no one was really going Jesus' way.

The church I grew up in had one message: "Jesus saves!" And we added nothing to it. We woke up, rinsed, came to church, and repeated it. I came to faith in a tradition that centered our living on Jesus' return. "He's coming soon! Get saved now! Time is running out!"

Salvation was on sale every Sunday, with the preacher extending his sweaty hand as if this was the last chance, the last time, the last call for salvation. The sky was always falling. Every instance of injustice, of crime and violence, of local and national corruption; every threat of planetary destruction, of war, of lust, of capitalistic consumption was used to drive home the point. "Time was winding up."

"Hurry up!" From sinners to saints, we needed to get our lives in order immediately. After our confession of faith, all we needed was a high school diploma and both baptism and marriage certificates. (A driver's license was optional for women.)

We just needed to be in a car with a bumper sticker that read, "Rapture ready." Because no matter the year, the political season or time of day, Jesus was always coming soon—in a cloud near you.[260] And there was nothing that we needed to do for a world that was "passing away." Just spread the word by asking the same question, the only question of everyone we met that day: "Do you know Jesus in the pardoning of your sins?" Because Jesus was coming; he just wasn't here yet.

Walter Brueggemann writes in *A Way Other Than Our Own*: "For I believe the crisis in the U.S. Church has most nothing to do with being liberal or conservative; it has everything to do with giving up on the faith and discipline of our Christian baptism and settling for a common, generic U.S. identity that is part patriotism, part consumerism, part violence and part affluence."[261] I would agree.

Buckle up. Take a ride with me while asking faithfully, "Are we there yet? Are we there yet? Are we there yet?" until there is no end in sight, until we identify with Christ, until we treat each other right for a "kin-dom" that is coming. And perhaps, get back in the water and ready ourselves to receive the baptism of the Holy Spirit and fire.

Questions

1. In Matthew 3:11, John said, "I baptize you with water for repentance." What does the North American church need to come clean about? What could be our confession?
2. Baptism suggests that "It all comes out in the wash." What then is our work as disciples?
3. What might the spiritual practices of accountability, forgiveness, healing, and reconciliation look like?
4. Believers go through the rinse cycle twice—a double baptism. What does it mean to be baptized with water and the Holy Spirit?

Lesson 3
1 Corinthians 12:13

The only fear is that those who have come into God's spiritual family and have drunk of the one Spirit will not let that Spirit have (the Spirit's) way in their lives. They may let human divisions take the place of oneness in the Spirit.[262]

T.B. Maston

The Bible and Race

Baptismal water is a drinking hole, a water fountain. Lap it up. Gulp it down. Guzzle it. Drink up. Because we need more water.

Let it wash over us and then come up good as new creatures in Christ Jesus. This is and we are good news. So don't be afraid of the water as it rises around us. Go down easy. Don't hold your nose.

Die quickly to what was in exchange for what will always be. "Made to drink of one Spirit," bottoms up. Let that reality rise in you, to be resurrected into one glorious body. Baptism offers new meaning and a way to live from the depths of our being.

It is the invitation that was extended to Christians in Corinth and to us who are reading: "For just as the body is one and has many members, and all the members of the body, though many, are one body, so it is with Christ. For in the one Spirit, we were all baptized into one body—Jews or Greeks, slaves or free—and we were all made to drink of one Spirit."

This is the "inward journey." Howard Thurman writes: "Whatever may be the occasion there comes a deep necessity which leads you finally into the closet with yourself. It is here that you raise the real questions about yourself. The leading one is, What is it, after all, that I amount to, ultimately? Such a question cuts through all that is superficial and trivial in life to the very nerve center of yourself. And this is a religious question because it deals with the total meaning of life at its heart. At such a moment, and at such a time, you must discover for yourself what is the true basis of your self-respect."[263]

It is an invitation to be Christ's body, his body, to embody his life here and now, to be the Word made flesh in our corner of the world.

Willie James Jennings is preparing us for life after this racialized reality in his book *After Whiteness: An Education in Belonging.* "The cultivation of belonging should be the goal of all education—not just any kind of belonging, but a profoundly creaturely belonging that performs the returning of the creature to the creator, and returning to an intimate and erotic energy that drives life together with God," he says.[264] As such, it is an opportunity to live fully and not through one category or another. Just be one.

Come alongside... Christ and his members and all other attachments come undone, no strings to pull, no strings attached but instead, a deep unwinding; rewinding time to take us back to the beginning when the waters hovered and created us out of the deep. In the beginning, there was only us. "Them" did not yet exist.

So, drink up. Let this awareness fill your cup to overflowing—until there is no distinction, until you cannot make out our differences. Until we are one body, drink up.

Questions

1. Baptismal waters and the Spirit's fountain, we get in and we also drink up. Why so much water? What do you make of this religious imagery?
2. Paul said to the believers at Corinth that the labels (cultural, experiential, and biological) are slippery when wet. What then does it mean to identify as a baptized believer?
3. More than water, what are we getting ourselves into when we get baptized?
4. What are baptized believers called to embody as members of one another and as members of Christ's resurrected body?
5. "One and the same Spirit," why is oneness, even in the Spirit, such a tight squeeze for Christians?
6. Dietrich Bonhoeffer wrote in his seminal work *Life Together*, "Because Christian community is founded solely on Jesus Christ, it is a spiritual and not a psychic reality. In this, it differs from all other communities." One body, one Spirit, how do these images inform our understanding of Christian community?
7. As baptized believers, what does the integration of this life look like? Feel like? Sound like?

LESSON 4
John 3:5

There is almost no teaching about race, as currently understood, in the great religious literatures of the world or in the writings of classical and medieval philosophers. For example, the Bible knows the term "race" only as a contest of speed or endurance. It has scores of references to "blood," and holds it in awe, but as the seat of the soul, the principle of life, rather than a physiological difference among men. The crowning affirmation about blood, in any event, is that "now in Christ Jesus you who once were far off have been brought near in the blood of Christ" (Eph. 2:13).[265]

Liston Pope
The Kingdom Beyond Caste

When we re-create human beings as races, it makes us easier to fit into the white supremacist capitalist machinery, which says we come in five colors. We are categorized for a color-coded hierarchy and written off as such for business purposes and for the American empire's use. But human being and belonging did not always only come in black and white; the meanings of good and evil were not always tucked under our skin.

To be sure, Europeans created a strong case for it. Naturalist George Louis Leclerc Buffon argued that "white" was "normative and the real and natural color of man." In his 1776 volume *On the Natural Varieties of Mankind*, Johann Friedrich Blumenbach, who coined the word Caucasian to describe the "white race," said there were five races: Caucasian, Mongoloid, Ethiopian, American, and Malay.[266] Swedish botanist, taxonomist, and zoologist, Carolus Linnaeus created binomial nomenclature and said human beings come in four varieties: Homo Europaeus, Homo Asiaticus, Homo Afer, and Homo Americanus. Georges Cuvier and John Hunter both counted three. Paul Topinard had nineteen and placed them under three headings. Edmund Burke managed to find sixty-three races.

Today, we count five different kinds of human beings—color-coded, sorted, and then stereotyped. These identities are not rooted in earth, dirt, soil, or country of origin as there is no white country, no black country, no red country, no yellow country, no brown country, no beige country. Where then do these colored people come from—because white is a color too? Their origin story is that of race. We are all re-created as people of color, which does not double as children of God.

Considering their travels, Europeans in the late seventeenth century began to view themselves as superior, referring to themselves as enlightened and renaming Africa the "Dark Continent" or the *terra nulla*. It was a Genesis 2 narrative. Race initially meant heredity, but Europeans would redefine it to depict themselves in the best light and re-create themselves as white. Europeans created a theory to support it, invented pseudo-scientific fields to prove it, wrote books to endorse it, stole a country it renamed the "New World" from its indigenous community and enslaved another for more than a century to demonstrate it.

The church fabricated theologies to center it, as if the gospel of Jesus Christ is about whiteness or white supremacy, which is heresy—because "all power belongs to God."[267] We believe that the *Imago Dei*, or the image of God, can be reduced to a color—as if we can color in God's face, as if any of us has seen the face of God and lived to talk about it. And all of this is somehow inspired by the Holy Spirit. Do we really believe this?

Because none of this is has anything to do with the "kin-dom" of God that Jesus was talking about. Yet, we have made it this and thereby racialized his gospel. We've gotten way off topic and away from Jesus' conversation with Nicodemus. For this, let us repent.

Jesus says that if we are to lay eyes on the "kin-dom" of God, then we must be born again of water and Spirit. Our skin and its social-coloring have nothing to do with it. Born from above, it all goes over Nicodemus' head and ours too if we are honest. Still, we are back at the water again and pushed forth by the Spirit of God.

Thus, we come through the water. We begin our new life by way of baptism, which offers Christian believers an opportunity to see ourselves afresh and as the unsegregated body of Christ—identified fully without the labels of race, class, or gender. Fresh out of the water, we are joined as his members. Consequently, this calls into question the North American church's alignment with race's color-coded caste system and its socially upheld power differences.

This watery grave is a dividing line. Baptism is the place where we cross over to the other side. It is the Lord's side. Its deep end is death. But without it, there is no new life. So, we grab a towel to go and die with Christ. When we rise, we speak again and yet for the first time as one born from above.

Questions

1. Why do we continue to racialize Jesus' gospel?
2. Why do we color in the face of God, paint Jesus into our corner of the world and then point to it as "a slice of heaven"?

3. What does it mean to be born from above, to be parented by way
   of the water and the Spirit?
4. Considering Jesus' conversation with Nicodemus, how should we
   talk about baptism?
5. What have you drawn from the water of baptism?

I hope these lessons won't mark the end of your engagement. Instead, continue to talk about baptism, race, and what you can draw from its waters, especially if you still have questions like Nicodemus. Someone once said, "The ground is level at the cross." The same can be said of the waters of baptism. Eye to eye with Jesus, you don't come up and look down your nose at anyone. But if you do, then what really drew you to the water?

CHAPTER 4
Drawing from the Water

Deep River, my home is over Jordan
Deep River, I want to cross over into campground.
Oh, don't you want to go to that Gospel feast,
That Promised Land where all is Peace?
Deep River.

John the Baptist got out of the boat, troubling the theology of persons unsuspecting. At least that is how Mark's gospel begins the story. Eugene Peterson reminds us in his book *Subversive Spirituality,* "The Gospel of Mark is the basic text for Christian spirituality. ... St. Mark, as the first Gospel, holds a certain primacy. No one had ever written a Christian gospel before Mark wrote his. He created a new genre."[268] And it is only "the beginning of the good news of Jesus Christ, the Son of God."

In fact, John the Baptist is merely fulfilling the prophecies of Isaiah[269] and Malachi[270]: "See, I am sending my messenger to prepare the way for me." John is then simply responding to a call, replying to an ad placed in the Old Testament. And his role is clear; his position is certain. John and Jesus, these leaping cousins, were ordained from the womb to partner in ministry.[271]

John begins to call the people together. "Excuse me. May I have your attention, please? The wait is over. What you are about to witness is the coming of the Messiah."

John is not just making an announcement but clearing the path before Jesus clears his throat. While it may not make Jesus' words easier to swallow, John is assisting the people in getting ready for who is to come. He is making sure that their ears are ready to hear. John the Baptist enters, saying, "Get ready. Get ready. Get ready."

The "kin-dom" of God is not only coming: it is near. John is not stalling, merely talking because the Lord is delayed. He is not trying to keep the people entertained or engaged—because there is some traffic pile-up in the heavens. He enters not as prophet but as preacher, not telling of a future time but speaking in the present tense: *God will be with us in the flesh.*

He will enter through a woman, through a vessel marked weak. The people will never look for him there. Her swollen belly will arouse no suspicion; the kingdom of darkness will feel no threat of danger, no warning signs, no alarms, no need to panic. It's just a woman.

Jesus will sneak in through the body cavity of one not searched for value. Because then and now, she is viewed as the mere property of another. Still, she will possess him. Immeasurable God in Mary, she will carry him. She will bring the Ancient of Days to term. We ask, "Mary did you know?" But only she really knows the whole story.

And if not for the angels, no one would believe her. Absent a phone booth, the Divine will change behind the curtain of a womb. Spirit draped in flesh, the people are looking for the roar of a king but he will enter with the cry of a child. They are watching the throne, waiting for God to make an entrance. Instead, he is traveling by way of a waddling woman with swollen feet, waiting for his time, waiting at the end of the line—an umbilical cord, waiting for the water to break, waiting to be born.

From Moses' wilderness to John's, the two men are known for making waves. John's will be a new Exodus, opening the floodgates to the way of the Lord. Dressed in camel's hair, he has an interesting fashion sense, but the prophet Ezekiel wore it first[272] and this will not be the last time that ministry begins in the wilderness. This will be Jesus' starting place, too.

Like Moses, John's baptismal waters provide a miraculous deliverance, a mystical escape from one life to the next. And now is not the time to be on the fence. We have run out of time to play it safe.

John starts shouting, "Make way! Make way! God is coming! God is coming! God is coming!"

And the message does more than trickle down. No, the people come from miles around. (I suspect the lines for baptism were longer than the ones we stand in for the latest I-Phone and largest flat screen televisions.) People come from Judea and Jerusalem to confess their sins and be baptized. Today that may not garner much celebration; but this is *good news* for them.

In fact, John causes quite a commotion and people take notice. He will not sit down and shut up. He does not stop preaching after the 11 a.m. service on Sunday. His message of the coming Lord troubles the waters and the minds of all who hear him.

John doesn't have to say anything, which makes the appeal even more alluring. He is in fact making trouble for himself, as there is already a king, Tiberius Caesar. Not long after Jesus enters, John exits, arrested for telling the story. And it is not just any story. John the Baptist's words change everything. The people needn't look up to the regional ruler, Herod, but look out for the soon-coming King, Jesus.

While we may have become accustomed to hearing it, choosing the Sundays we can skip because we have heard enough, or we know the story well enough, the ruler in John the Baptist's day had had enough. Because this was not the same old story. Eugene Peterson wrote about the Bible,

> Within the large, capacious context of the biblical story, we learn to think accurately, behave morally, preach passionately, sing joyfully, pray honestly, obey faithfully. But we dare not abandon the story as we do any or all of these things, for the minute we abandon the story, we reduce reality to the dimensions of our minds and feelings and experience. The moment we formulate doctrines, draw up our moral codes, and throw ourselves into a life of ministry apart from a continuous re-immersion in the story itself, we walk right out of the presence and activity of God and set up our own shop.[273]

This is why we gather. We come to be re-immersed in the story, to soak our souls in the river Jordan, to fill our lives with the cleansing and transformative waters of baptism. We don't leave this sanctuary to make a splash. No, we enter the story and stand next to John the Baptist to cry out, "Prepare the way of the Lord, make his paths straight." Because we, too, have come to make waves.

Race is the issue—not human beings. It is a bad social prescription; it is the lens, not the image. The sociopolitical construct, which fluctuates in meaning, will never produce relational stability. Instead, baptism, the waters that trouble all othering and power-based identities and from which the raceless gospel can be drawn, offers an ontology—a way of being—that draws us together as next of kin for an undivided "kin-dom" that is coming.

The sociopolitical construct of race continues to influence and inform every American institution and faith tradition. Race is ubiquitous. It seems impossible to get it out of our minds and off our bodies. For many persons, there is a sense that we will never rid ourselves of it. Hearing no prophetic objections to the contrary, it seems the North American church would agree.

Still, there is a growing restlessness, a dis-ease for many people who have grown tired of the personal, social, and spiritual assumptions, restrictions, and even privileges of race. Debra Dickerson captures this reality in her book *The End of Blackness*, writing that "blackness, as it has come to be understood, is rapidly losing its ability to describe, let alone to predict or manipulate, the political and social behavior of African Americans. Given its strictures and the limitations it places upon the growth and free will of those to whom it refers, it diminishes their sovereignty as rational and moral actors."[274] While Dickerson is arguing for a new revised version of blackness, the global church must question its continued use of racialized identities and theologies.

I believe in the water and its witness, its ability to draw out all our impurities, to drown out all the competing voices so that we can be our true selves, our new selves, as members of Christ's body. Some of us may be familiar with the expression, "They called me everything but a child of God." In baptism, the believer is exactly that: able to claim God as next of kin. How then did some Christians think that race would be able to deny this divine parentage? The hymnist sang, "Take me to the water to be baptized." The answer is there.

Baptism, the witness of water and the Holy Spirit, is not a good scrub but "the cleansing flood." Water rising above our heads, this ritual of baptism renders us dead to one life and alive to the next. Citizens of an undivided "kin-dom" that is coming, we are taken to the water. The portal of new life in Jesus the Christ, our Savior, we take from the waters an uncategorical way of being and only faint memories of who we once were, never to be heard from again. We are called by a new name and are identified by, in, and through Christ's body only.

Baptism was of primary importance to Jesus' ministry and is the universal sign of a Christian. It is subversion by immersion, undermining the systems and structures that once held power over the new believer as one goes under. This is not a religious habit, merely our obedience to the way Jesus did it. But it is the way of Jesus, evidence that we are following in his footsteps. Consequently, a certificate of baptism is not evidence of a finished work and should not be treated as a blue ribbon for righteousness. No, as we read in 1 Corinthians 15, we Christians die daily. Our former selves were not meant to survive.

This truth needs to be coupled with a mystical spirituality of "somebodiness." Not to be confused with celebrity status or self-righteousness, there is a need for a deep sense of knowing who we are as human beings. This is not a new idea but a renewed call for an ontology—the nature of being and becoming—that we don't have to buy into. It is the unequivocal self-awareness that I am somebody. Not a packaged deal, it is not a sermon series with three points and neat alliterations, or seven steps to becoming a better version of ourselves. Instead, it is an embodied practice of faith that is aligned with who we have always been: children of God.

On April 26, 1967, Martin Luther King Jr. asked the student body at Glenville High School in Cleveland, Ohio, to cultivate their self-worth. On October 26, 1967, he spoke to students at Barratt Junior High School in Philadelphia, Pennsylvania. In his speech titled "What Is Your Life's Blueprint?" he said: "Number one in your life's blueprint should be a deep belief in your own dignity, your own worth, and your own somebodiness. Don't allow anybody to make you feel that you are nobody. Always feel that you count. Always feel that you have worth. And always feel that your life has ultimate significance."

"I am somebody." This statement was later popularized by Jesse Jackson, who shared a poem titled "I am—Somebody," written by William Holmes Borders Sr., during an episode of *Sesame Street* in 1972. The poem concludes, "I am God's child. I am somebody." I wasn't even alive then and, to be fair, the sentiment of this self-declaration goes farther back than this. The need for self-awareness has been discussed by biblical figures, philosophers, preachers, poets, and artists alike.

David wrote about this self-knowledge: "You desire truth in the inward being; therefore, teach me wisdom in my secret heart" (Ps. 51:6). Jesus invited persons who judged others to self-reflect: "Why do you see the speck in your neighbor's eye, but do not notice the log in your own eye?" (Matt. 7:3). And, legend has it that the two words, "Know thyself," were carved in stone at the entrance to Apollo's temple at Delphi in Greece.

"Knowing yourself is the beginning of all wisdom," Aristotle believed. French theologian and reformer John Calvin made this connection in 1536: "There is no deep knowing of God without a deep knowing of self, and no deep knowing of self without a deep knowing of God." "Our vocation is not simply to be, but to work together with God in the creation of our own life, our own identity, our own destiny," Thomas Merton, a Trappist monk, wrote in *New Seeds of Contemplation*. He told readers to "pray for our own discovery." Consequently, Toni Morrison's words are my sentiments exactly. "Don't let anybody, anybody convince you this is the way the world is and therefore must be. It must be the way it ought to be," Morrison wrote in *The Source of Self-Regard: Selected Essays, Speeches, and Meditations*.

Recently, I was invited to the University of Mississippi for a conversation on race, anti-racism, and beloved community. During the Q&A period, Sonia, an African American neurosurgeon, shared that her patients were experiencing poverty and, quite frankly, while she could appreciate my position intellectually, she wondered how it could be practically applied in a racialized society. A brain surgeon, she understood the concept of racelessness, of seeing oneself outside of the "white gaze," of existing apart from the categorizations of race, but the crippling conditions of poverty coupled with racism made it hard to believe that it was indeed possible for her patients. She wanted to know how she could make this moderated discussion in a university classroom a reality. With several follow-up questions, she continued to press me on it. She argued that her patients' social condition doesn't afford them days off to do the work of self-actualization.

In that moment I was reminded that while I speak from a deep sense of knowing who I am apart from race, many of us need to be reminded that "I am somebody." This "I am" statement is a cure-all for me and speaks to an inward orientation that is not dependent on external factors or the fluctuating opinions of others. With the trappings of capitalism, sexism, racism, and militarism, human beings rely heavily on external signs of success and self-worth: You are what you have. You are worth as much as you possess or have amassed. Personal validation has been outsourced to things and other people.

"She's going to be *somebody*." "He is *somebody* you should know!" While Christians espouse the view that we are all God's children, too often we point to those who have gifts or talents we value. Saying that everyone is somebody is not comparable to giving everyone a trophy for merely existing; instead, it is treating everyone as valuable regardless of their contributions to society.

Drawn from the water, the raceless gospel is rooted in a mystical spirituality of "somebodiness," a belief in indivisible individuality or selfhood apart from "ruling relationships" that maintain social hierarchies. This aligns with the early church's first creed: "For you are children of God in the Spirit. There is no Jew or Greek; there is no slave or free; there is no male and female. For you are all on one in the Spirit." It is a message that bears repeating. So, repeat after me a summary of the raceless gospel: "I am God's child. I am somebody."

Christians are Spirit-filled people, Pentecostal people, multilingual people, all members of the body of Christ and thus, all equal and children of God—though race calls us people of color. But race has no place in our ecclesiology. Because for race, there is only one true color: white. Consequently, only one category of people is guaranteed membership and belonging in the body of Christ. It is an aesthetic righteousness (that is, color of skin, texture of hair, shape of eyes, size of nose) that eliminates those folks who will never be "white enough."

The gospel is raceless. Through the power of the Holy Spirit and by way of the water, the early church was able to put aside their differences. People came from all over the world to form this new community. The experience in the upper room at Pentecost in Acts 2 is the first example of an integrated sacred space. The book of Acts also demonstrates the unifying power of the water: "Can anyone withhold the water for baptizing these people who have received the Holy Spirit just as we have?"[275]

While the early church did wrestle with cultural inclusion at the council at Jerusalem, as recorded in Acts 15, revelations given by the Holy Spirit made the gospel's goal clear: "And God, who knows the human heart, testified to them by giving them the Holy Spirit, just as he did to us; and cleansing their hearts by faith (God) has made no distinction between us and them."[276] This had already been debated and resolved at the Council of Jerusalem with Peter and Paul, Simeon and James. These differences were settled in Christ and through our baptismal identity; we are new creatures, erasing all that we were back then. All these divisions are brought together in him. Jesus consumes them all when we go down in the waters with him, hatchets and hatreds buried

Likewise, we are saved by faith through grace—not according to the sociopolitical construct of race. The early church lived countercultural to ancient society. In similar fashion, the North American church is called to live in opposition to this color-coded caste system rooted in the pigments of our imagination. The church was not meant to be a segregated, mono-lingual, culturally assimilated, one "race" per sacred space reality. But this invitation is not new. The Spirit keeps calling us through poets such as Lucile Clifton who said, "flesh is the coat we unfasten / And throw off."[277] Educator, scholar, and pathbreaking feminist bell hooks implored us to let skin be skin again: "The skin I'm in / The skin I'm in / Is just a covering / It cannot tell my story."[278]

Theologian Willie James Jennings is preparing us for life after this racialized reality, writing in *After Whiteness: An Education in Belonging* that "The cultivation of belonging should be the goal of all education—not just any kind of belonging, but a profoundly creaturely belonging that performs the returning of the creature to the creator, and returning to an intimate and erotic energy that drives life together with God." Because if religion, if Christianity does not have the power to deliver us from this color-coded hierarchy, from racialized discrimination and injustice, then who are we learning to be and what kind of salvation are we talking about? If the church in North America cannot unify as the body of Christ, then what are we saying about Jesus' gospel? Because baptism should always have rippling effects.

Race permeates all American life. That the same can be said of the spiritual life is evidence of theological malpractice, as race changes the means and nature of salvation. The preoccupation with the social-coloring of skin is a modern example of self-absorption and the language of the North American empire, which should have never been adopted by the Christian faith. "One Lord, one faith, one baptism,"[279] yet North American Christians continue to draw lines when it comes to race. A visible representation of an unanswered prayer of Jesus,[280] not even on Sunday morning do his followers gather as his body.

Race is a social problem that is fixed only with its removal as a fixture of human identity, not to be tinkered with and made to work despite its history of dehumanization. There is a need for a paradigm shift that moves us beyond anti-racism. W.E.B. DuBois names the work explicitly: "Nevertheless, here are some social problems before us demanding careful study, questions awaiting satisfactory answers. We must study, we must investigate, we must attempt to solve; and the utmost that the world can demand is, not lack of human interest and moral conviction, but rather the heart-quality of fairness, and an earnest desire for the truth despite its possible unpleasantness."[281]

It is this work that I am committed to because I believe in the water of baptism and that the presentation of a certificate of baptism is misleading. The work toward an inward orientation that not only changes our perspective—that is "the renewal of (the) mind"[282]—but also challenges the systems that support social othering, marginalization and invisibility remains unfinished.

Baptism both addresses race and is a response to its progeny, namely segregation, and the racism that justifies it. George D. Kelsey wrote in *Racism and the Christian Understanding of Man*: "Since racism assumes some segments of humanity to be defective in essential being, and since for Christians all being is from the hand of God, racism alone among the idolatries calls into question the divine creative action."[283] Consequently, the North American church needs to be taken back to the water and its beginning with the only body it was expected to reflect. "Worse than being evil is being inauthentic," writes Andrew Root in *Faith Formation in a Secular Age*.[284] But as long as the North American church remains segregated, it will be just that.

While artists[285] and authors[286] cast visions of a post-racial society and church and social justice activists call for reparations, many North American Christians gloss over the issue of race and subsequently class, gender, and neocolonial capitalism. They call for forgiveness and reconciliation without providing proof of the work it takes to offer and express either. Just look inside a church building on any given Sunday and you will find that it largely embodies neither in terms of the sociopolitical construct of race. After the death of George Floyd in Minneapolis, Minnesota, many people said that America was experiencing a "racial reckoning" and with that, the problems of race were front and center again. Still, the majority of Americans wondered if focusing on race would solve our problems.[287] Nevertheless, the North American church, still towing "the color line," represents a lost opportunity to demonstrate through embodiment what unity and a reconciled community could look like.

Why is it taking the North American church so long to change itself and to change the world around it? Is the work of baptism not an instant reminder that we are children of God?[288] The Christian scriptures offer a new narrative, a new kind of human being and belonging in the world. It is equally critical and essential that Jesus' followers embody his teachings and ministry, which began in the water of baptism. This new community is formed after drowning out the power-grabbing ideologies of capitalism, identity politics, militarism, neocolonialism, patriarchy, and race. While it has been used as a tool by both the oppressor and the oppressed, "the Bible is not a fixed, frozen, readily exhausted read; it is rather a 'script,' always reread through which the Spirit makes new," Walter Brueggemann wrote in *Struggling with Scripture.*[289] For the raceless gospel as a baptismal pedagogy to emerge to desegregate the church in North America, there will be both internal and external struggling.

Desegregation in public spaces in the United States came after protest during the Civil Rights Movement of the 1950s and 60s. Likewise, the raceless gospel that takes the North American church to the water of baptism is pushing back on a racialized narrative. It is as Alice Walker said, "We are the ones we have been waiting for."[290] These racialized identities—that is beige (mixed race), black, brown, red, yellow, and white—don't go down in the water easily or quietly. Still, nothing less than full submersion is required for a unified embodiment of faith in Jesus.

Since Paul's writings were also used to justify and promote the enslavement of African and Indigenous people[291] along with the oppression of women, which continues to impact relationships still based on "relationships of ruling,"[292] we do not take the scriptures' use lightly. Consequently, the baptismal waters would also double as a reflection pool. A shared experience of most Christian believers, it presents an opportunity for the baptized believer to see oneself from its perspective. Words drawn from the waters of baptism, these texts had long emerged as a way forward. The lens provided by Galatians 3:28 has helped historic figures such as Mary McLeod Bethune: "With these words the scales fell from my eyes and the light came flooding in. My sense of inferiority, my fear of handicaps, dropped away: 'Whosoever,' it said. No Jew nor Gentile... no black nor white; just 'whosoever.' It meant that I, a humble Negro girl, had just as much chance as anybody in the sight and love of God."[293]

Galatians 3:27-28 casts a beautiful vision to work toward, and Colossians 3:9-11 affirms its reality. The letter to the Galatians was written by Paul, "a hard-line nationalist Jew [who became] the founder of multiethnic communities." N.T Wright says of Paul, "[W]hat he said about Jesus, and about God, the world and what it meant to be genuinely human was creative and compelling—and controversial, in his own day and ever after. Nothing would ever be quite the same."[294] Paul was the murderer of Christians turned missionary, whose heart, soul, and mind were changed when he realized that he was persecuting Christ himself. It reminds me of the words of Jesus, "Truly I tell you, just as you did it to one of the least of these who are members of my family, you did it to me."[295]

From finger pointer to pillar of the community, Paul wrote from experience. From one-sided faith to all-including, this cultured, "member of the people of Israel" and "tribe of Benjamin," this "Hebrew of the Hebrews"[296] and well-educated bigot, a good guy according to the law, who took his faith seriously, Paul thought he knew and had seen it all. No water baptism but scaled eyes, he was given a new vision of humanity and never saw things the same way again. This Paul—whose name was changed in his encounter and who went from the persecutor to the persecuted; who served in coat check while Stephen was being stoned; who was converted, changed, and born again—wrote: "As many of you as we baptized into Christ have clothed yourselves with Christ, there is no longer Jew or Greek, there is no longer slave or free, there is no longer male and female; for all of you are one in Christ Jesus" (Gal. 3:27-28). Likewise, I write to the church in North America: As many of you as were baptized into Christ have clothed yourselves with Christ, there is no longer beige nor black people, there is no longer brown nor red people, there is no longer white nor yellow people; for all of you are one in Christ Jesus.

This is the work of baptism. It is not a dunking contest or a numbers game. No exclusion and no exclusivity, whoever we were and whatever we did is now water under the bridge. Baptism washes us of our past and of these categories. The rules of this baptismal pool require that there be no running back to our old ways. Instead, "in Christ, we live, move, and have our being."[297]

The North American church sends a conflicting message. Baptism is open to all, and the pool cancels membership to groups that require othering. In his "Open Letter to the Born Again," James Baldwin noted the difference: "The people who call themselves 'born again' today have simply become members of the richest, most exclusive private club in the world, a club that man from Galilee could not possibly hope—or wish—to enter."[298] This baptismal water should trouble us and should cause trouble for all other identities.

Galatians 3:28 is the early church's first creed and likely was written in response to an ancient cliché: "I thank God every day that I was born a native, not a foreigner; free and not a slave; a man and not a woman."[299] Paul did not accommodate this view, adapt his Christology, or conform them to fit neatly into these pre-packaged ways to exist. He did not bless or baptize these categories. He didn't check these boxes.

Paul also did not shy away from nationalism, bigotry, slavery, and sexism. Never dead issues, they can be argued as something that Christianity is dead set against. Dead with Christ, baptism is a eulogy. Baptism rids us of false binaries. No more battles of the sexes, culture wars, or us-versus-them mythology. Because whoever we used to be—our physicality; all our history, memory, responsibilities, and loyalties; our allegiances and alliances—all of our body's identities float to the top, dead in the water.

The raceless gospel for a baptismal pedagogy could act as a catalyst for desegregating sacred spaces. It would need only to be repeated. Like the call to discipleship, extended after a sermon, baptized believers need to be reminded of their new life in Jesus. Congregational leaders could center this symbolic act that has real world implications.

Along with *lectio divina* and fasting and praying, baptism should be treated as an ongoing spiritual practice. It both *forms* and *informs* our faith. Baptism is a means of connecting with God and likewise other believers. As with Jesus' baptism, it can result in our hearing from God the reminder of our relatedness to the Divine.

While not an escape from the body, baptism is a declaration of its otherworldliness. It is as Thomas Ryan said when talking of the incarnation of Jesus in *Reclaiming the Body in Christian Spirituality*, "In the face of our devaluations of the flesh that embodies God and the earth which is God's home, God sent us a message: from now on, I am identified with this bodiliness, this fleshiness, this materiality, this sensuality, this worldliness, this passion."[300] So, we must be critical and mindful of the words used to describe these bodies. Our human being must be reclaimed from race.

The raceless gospel offers a "nondual consciousness," evidenced by Jesus' baptism wherein the line between heaven and earth did not exist. One's baptismal identity if lived into can be an expression of heaven on earth, then, that is unity with God and peace with neighbor. "It is a vision that, by definition, is beyond the dualities of human language and the linear, dualistic, chopped up consciousness through which almost all humans now see the world," wrote Jim Marion in *Putting on the Mind of Christ*.[301] In the Christian tradition, it is referred to as the "beatific vision of God" on earth. The raceless gospel prophesies deliverance[302] from the false binaries of race. We need only take on more water until the water takes us over.

Thomas Merton understood the recreation made possible through baptism, as he wrote in *The New Man*:

> The Christian view does not make an abstract division between matter and spirit. It plunges into the existential depths of the concrete union of body and soul which makes up the human person, and by clearing the spiritual temple of all those ways of thinking which obstruct our inward vision, opens the way to an existential communion at the same time with ourselves and with God in the actual, subsisting, spiritual reality of our own inviolable being. In this way, the body is not discarded (which is in any case not possible) but elevated and spiritualized.[303]

Fresh from the water of baptism, a desegregated church would return to the "Spirit hovering over water" identity, namely as children of God and thereby next of kin to all human beings. Because who told you that you were a colored person—that is beige, black, brown, red, yellow, or white? A racialized identity alienates Christian believers from God, making them question their identity and call into question their relatedness to other human beings—because "if you are not skin to me, then you are not kin to me."[304]

Race not only changes how we view ourselves and others but also how we identify with and talk to God. *Parrhesia*, the freedom of speech between human beings and God ceases to exist when one's God-given identity is called into question. The sociopolitical construct of race is to blame for talking us out of and away from the water. "It is my belief that in the Presence of God, there is neither male nor female, white or black, Gentile or Jew, Protestant nor Catholic, Hindu, Buddhist, nor Muslim but a human spirit stripped to the literal substance of itself before God," wrote Howard Thurman in *The Creative Encounter*.[305] It is no doubt then that, apart from centering itself in baptism, the North American church will continue to behave like a fish out of water, segregated and unable to come together as the body of Christ.

Second-century theologian Tertullian said, "we, little fishes, after the image of our Ichthys, Jesus Christ, are born in the water." The raceless gospel is then a proclamation of homecoming, of reunion, of assembly. It is also cause for singing:

> Heaven bell a-ring, I know de road,
> Heaven bell a-ring, I know de road;
> Heaven bell a-ring, I know de road,
> Jesus sittin' on de waterside
>
> Do come along, do let us go,
> Do come along, do let us go,
> Do come along, do let us go,
> Jesus sittin' on de waterside.[306]

Chapter 5

Baptism as Reflection Pool

And before I'll be a slave,
I'll be buried in my grave
And go home to my Lord
And be free

And at that self-same moment, ye died and were born; and the Water of
salvation was at once your grave and your mother.[307]

St. Cyril of Jerusalem

If [the human being] is in the likeness of God, and rules the whole
earth, and has been granted authority over everything on earth from God,
who [can be] his buyer, tell me? Who [can be] his seller? To God alone
belongs this power; or rather, not even God himself. For his gracious gifts,
it says, are irrevocable (Rom. 11:29). God would not therefore reduce the
human race to slavery, since he himself, when we had been enslaved to sin,
spontaneously recalled us to freedom. But if God does not enslave what is
free, who is he that sets his own power above God's?

Gregory of Nyssa
Homily IV on Ecclesiastes

A-racial anthropology… Pre-racial ecclesiology… Pre-racial (liberation)
theology… The race-less gospel… Throughout this journey I have
referred to my writings under all these terms, all of which seek to address
and outright attack the "epidermalization of inferiority."[308] They did not
come to me all at once and neither did this idea of racelessness. When I
began to think critically about my identity in college, I had every intention
of being "black and proud."

But when I learned that Carolus Linnaeus had invented these color-coded
categories for human beings and that no one from the African diaspora had
a hand in it, then I decided that I needed to undermine it. I later developed
a strong dislike for race and a natural inclination to interrogate it. I just
couldn't accept its terms and conditions for living in American society.

I wasn't trying to create something new or different, though my initial
writings did challenge the anthropology ("Anthropologically during slavery,
European Americans argued that their biological characteristics were superior
and more pleasing to the eye aesthetically—thereby claiming whiteness

as the image of God."[309]), theology, and ecclesiology that were created in response to American slavery. I tried talking to a few people about how I was feeling about race, but the conversations were always the same. No one could offer me a way out of race. For them, it just wasn't possible or feasible.

"This is the white man's world: We just live in it." Evidence of being socialized within a white supremacist educational system and thus developing a racialized worldview, they just couldn't see themselves outside of race's view of them. There was no place outside of the "white gaze," which made sense given America's history.

Their conclusion wasn't defeatist but the reality of the so-called New World where bodies racialized as black received less-than-fair treatment from the American government and its leaders and citizens. Dwight N. Hopkins observed in *Down, Up and Over: Slave Religion and Black Theology* that "Presidents Washington, Jefferson, Madison, Monroe, and Jackson were all slaveholders. Hero of the War of 1812, Andrew Jackson 'saw the profitability of the slave-labor system as evidence of its moral integrity.' Thirteen of the first fifteen presidents were Southerners who held blacks as private chattel or Northerners who supported black legal subordination."[310]

The church and its denominations didn't fare any better, even after slavery ended: "With the end of slavery, most white denominations quickly retreated to old positions, joining the rest of the white society in supporting and practicing segregation."[311]

Endorsed and supported legally, socially, and theologically, there was no way I should have doubted it. Slavery loitered in language. It could be argued that I had no reason to question it. But the more I learned about race, the more questions came regarding its validity and authority. Race was the problem—not me.

Despite it being a choice within human control, powerlessness had been ingrained and was a part of what the creators and enforcers of race had in mind. It was an acceptable part of the culture. Sidney M. Mintz and Richard Price provided this insight in *The Birth of African-American Culture: An Anthropological Perspective*:

> But the European master's institutional ideal was a colonial society in which no such interpenetration occurred, since merging or boundary-crossing of any kind might eventually erode the principles of coercion of any upon which the whole colonial undertaking rested. Though rarely voiced in any explicit detail, it is clear that the European colonists hoped for the "acculturation" of slave populations to a total acceptance of slave status—and surely many

of them believed that proper methods, unrelenting discipline, and enough time would bring this about.[312]

Africans racialized as black were expected to be all slave or nothing at all. Race doesn't have a middle ground, a shared rung on the ladder of human hierarchy, that "Great Chain of Being," and there was never a plan to reconcile our differences. No, part of the colonial design included a way out of subordination: "slaves for life" was the mission. Consequently, accepting a racial identity would equate to acculturation, to maintain my membership within a colonial society.

Had I known, I would never have agreed to this: "Black men want to prove to white men, at all costs, the richness of their thought, the equal value of their intellect."[313] As a result, more questions came. How had this sociopolitical construct of oppression, which is both structural and behavioral, been introduced to me? How did I come to be known as black, and did I want to continue my relationship with this social identity?

Would I be viewed as a "race traitor" if I did? Black is a category that became an identity, which created a culture of survival from white supremacy. But the word also served to tongue-tie those racialized as black to the oppressive condition of the marginalized so much so that you could not talk about transcendence unless it was heaven in "the sweet by and by." But I wanted to be free in the here and now.

Did I have to be black, or was there some other way of being in the world? Social not biological, why couldn't I simply reject the argument that race was essential since it historically and presently denied persons of African ancestry full personhood? Race would always transgress against me. Was there an opt-out clause, and would people understand this soulish longing for solidarity with my inner self who was telling me that this was not who she ever was or wanted to be?

These questions were creating a soul boundary. Race had gone too far, and I decided race would remain a superficial descriptor and only skin deep. It would not get to the deepest parts of me. My life would be a rebuttal and I would reject all forms and attempts to color me in, including person of color. Because what was I identifying with? Robert Jensen answers this question in *The Heart of Whiteness: Confronting Race, Racism, and White Privilege*:

> But politically, white is not just white, of course. White is power. And using the terms white/non-white reminds us of that. What do people of color have in common? That is, what makes the category "people of color" make

sense? The only commonality is that the people in that category are on the subordinated side of white supremacy. Nothing intrinsically links people of indigenous, African, Latino, and Asian descent in the United States except their common experience of being targeted, abused, and victimized—albeit in different ways at different times—by white-supremacist society. Take that experience away, and the category of "people of color" vanishes. The people, of course, don't vanish, nor does their color change. But nothing links them except the experience of oppression. And the group perpetrating that oppression is white, another socially created category defined by power.[314]

Racialized identities will always support white supremacy. There is no way around it.

Brian Bantum provided yet another helpful definition that aided in my repositioning of race in *Redeeming Mulatto: A Theology of Race and Christian Hybridity*, writing,

> Race is a phenomenon of racial performance that forms disciples. Race is not merely a form of social organization, but more significantly a form of religious expression and identity that shape who a person is. But race as a system of belief also indicates more than who a person is. Structures of racial formation articulate the telos of the inhabitant's life, what she will live into, and what she will not. In this regard race becomes a category that organizes and guides the very presumptions people make about themselves and their world. However, this performance of race remains, the ways it is lived into and acted out of, hidden even in the midst of competing visions of racial life.[315]

Once I saw race for what it was and would always be to me, I couldn't unsee it. Race was not a self-revelation or a given but a hand-me-down identity thousands of years too small.

The realization is not uncommon, this real experience of race defining every single moment of our lives and the ongoing internal struggle with racialized or color-coded identities. Emily Bernard shared her story in *Black Is the Body: Stories from My Grandmother's Time, My Mother's Time, and Mine*:

> My brown daughters became black when they were six years old. They were watching television one day in February, Black History Month. A commercial came on. It was more like a thirty-second history lesson, a commemoration of a pilot, a poet, or a politician; a First Black, as a writer I know calls them. *Them* being the racial pioneers, the inaugural Negroes,

the foremost African Americans to break through racial barriers in their chosen fields. By 'break through," I mean, of course, secure the regard of white people.

"See, we're black," Giulia said to Isabella.

"No, we're brown," Isabella responded.

"Yeah, but they call it black," Giulia explained.

Despite my efforts to shield them, my daughters had somehow gotten wise to the absurd and illogical nature of American racial identity. Blackness, Giulia had figured out, had nothing to do with actual skin color.[316]

Bernard continued explaining that, of course, race was not something we saw though we say it. We were not, in fact, talking about color but a shared social condition of the minoritized, marginalized, and oppressed.

Not surprisingly, this is not new. The renaming of Africans and the re-creation of their image has a long and derogatory history. Heathen, colored, Negro, and black: all these names have a negative connotation. David Brion Davis wrote in *The Problem of Slavery in Western Culture*,

> For reasons that can perhaps never be explained, it was the African's color of skin that became his defining characteristic, and aroused the deepest response in Europeans. Though often designated as a "Moor" or "Ethiopian," he was also a "negro" to the Spanish and Portuguese, a "noir" to the French, and a "black" to the English; in all four languages the word carried the connotation of gloom, evil, baseness, wretchedness, and misfortune.[317]

Once these words landed on their would-be oppressors' tongues, Africans were uprooted from their own. These names and the meanings they claimed were as naturally obvious as their justification for American slavery.

So, I had to get away from them. I wanted bodily autonomy, full self-realization, self-mastery, and self-consciousness outside of and apart from the stereotypes of race, white supremacy (because race serves only to justify white supremacy), and its progeny. Also, the binary approach of moving from white supremacy ("white power") to black supremacy ("black power"), wherein goodness and right behavior are switched between the two groups, maintained the struggle for race-based domination. An endless call and response, a person would still need to overvalue one and undervalue the other. I needed an alternative way to look at race to live into a new narrative that claimed my country of origin, my culture, and my heritage while deracializing my existence and decentering whiteness. If not, I would spend the rest of my life within the confine of the so-called white imagination.

It seemed like a lot of work to just call myself an African American, but there was more to it. Karenga explained it succinctly: "A Negro is from nowhere. You call a man from Germany a German-American, a man from Japan a Japanese-American, and a man from Mexico a Mexican-American. The so-called 'Negro' if he is from anywhere is from Africa. If he lives in the United States, he is an Afro-American."[318] Consequently, I would no longer be colonized as black, live as if under unending surveillance and scrutiny, and would exorcise internalized white supremacy. I didn't know then that I was working out my salvation, with the raceless gospel becoming a part of an underground railroad for race abolitionists. I wanted deliverance from this black-white world, and I was certain that there were others yet to be discovered and that I could have a hand in creating.

Still, I know that my words will not be legible to everyone. Early on, I shared with a close family member that I wanted to identify as an African American and the response was so verbally abusive that I never spoke about it again. Instead, I started writing and filled journal after journal with my questions, ruminations, and initial findings. I started collecting articles and newspaper clippings, new and rare books on race and its progeny. I read book after book, collecting sentences that created its own paper trail. Some would say it became an obsession. But I needed to know everything there was to know about race's origin and history.

Due to these questions and so many others, I found myself in an unfamiliar place, but it wasn't unknown territory.[319] "But my purpose was different: What I want to do is help the black man to free himself from the arsenal of complexes that has been developed by the colonial environment," Frantz Fanon wrote in *Black Skin, White Masks*.[320] I now had the eyes to see it. I was already committed to writing the blog, at the time called "The Daily Race" and today, racelessgospel.com, when I realized what I had to say. But I was so afraid of what it would mean for me. Was there life after race?

It took more than a decade to get the water of baptism, and now you can't pull me out of it. The raceless gospel is a moral assignment. For me, there is no need to assert that there is value and dignity in all human beings. That we are all God's children makes it a given. Our ecclesiology needs to be liberated from race and its progeny. This is just one opportunity.

None of this is easy—for anyone. (Perhaps I should have said that at the start.) This work is for explorers, for stuntpeople, for risk-takers. It is not for religious experts but disciples, pilgrims, and apprentices. It's going to take time and lots of practice. Let me be clear: I cannot see past Jesus' feet, so I am learning as I go, and this is an invitation to walk with me.

Lord knows it can be hard to see the "kin-dom" that is coming. Employing the words of Friedrich Nietzsche, Eugene Peterson describes discipleship as "a long obedience in the same direction." He wrote in a book of the same name, "A person has to be thoroughly disgusted with the way things are to find the motivation to set out on this Christian way."[321] Yes, we all begin dissatisfied with what we know and crave to know something different, something more. For me, I want to shake things up when it comes to race. But no one really knows what goes into a world turned upside down.

The raceless gospel is equal parts calling, conviction, and holy longing. But sabotaging the plans of white supremacy is well worth it in the end, especially if you can look at yourself without the lens of race and its socially prescribed prejudices. Oh, how I live for the future of this deracialized reality, where everyone is someone and no one is actively trying to make us something other than this.

But race has not been fully submerged in the water, and we must reflect on this. Why does it keep coming up? Because it is not dead in the water. Instead, we have made it synonymous with our bodies and the body of Christ.

As baptized believers, we speak from submerged places of being. We go down in the deep and into dark spaces where human beings do not live. We go down into water with mammals—sharks, seahorses, whales, octopuses, and schools of fish. We go down deep where the Spirit hovers and calls us children of God. We come up from the water, and we must answer to it.

The raceless gospel is proof that change has come. Viewing baptism as a reflection pool, I now see race with new eyes, and I hope you will too. Degrading bodies racialized as black while elevating others racialized as white, race supports an unbalanced power dynamic, masquerading as identity. But the true work of race is not mysterious, as those who are at the bottom of this color-coded pyramid scheme can see it clearly.

Further, Jesus didn't come up from the water with an air of superiority or a claim of supremacy. Instead, God claimed him as family, my beloved son. And Jesus didn't call his followers to walk away from the marginalized and minoritized. Instead, "Jesus reached beyond his people, beyond his perceived mandate, beyond his tradition, extending himself to the 'other.' … All of us to some extent, hold the line against 'the other.' All of us, to some extent, know that our faith calls us out beyond that," wrote Walter Brueggemann in *A Way Other Than Our Own*.[322] Those early Christians knew that their place was with everyone. Not a building but a community, they sought to build up everyone.

The raceless gospel, rooted in baptismal identity, is an embodied ecclesiology that aims to drown out all competing identities. It is an expression of a creed, recorded in Galatians 3:27-28. Paul says, "As many of you as were baptized into Christ have clothed yourselves with Christ. There is no longer Jew or Greek; there is no longer slave or free; there is no longer male and female, for all of you are one in Christ Jesus."

One body, all members of each other, we are not identified by culture, class, or gender but by the Word made flesh that transcends all descriptions. We are not members of a racialized body but a Spirit-filled one—Pentecostal people, multilingual, all equal, crossing cultures and no one off the list. Tongues of fire, we are baptized by water and the Spirit. We talk different.

So, what's the word for human beings not living by the skin of their teeth or according to the social-coloring of skin? What's the word for people living outside of color-coded categories and without being colored in? What's the word for a message that declares there is no us and them, where no one is out and everyone is in—because we're all next of kin? It's the raceless gospel, and it was Jesus' intent that the tip of our tongues be a diving board into a deeper and wider way of human being and belonging. I'm just here to coax it out of you. Come on, baptized believer, and say it.

The raceless gospel requires us to deconstruct race and to decolonize identity. It begins with the way we speak about ourselves, our neighbor, and our God. I invite you to tear down the linguistic, legal, and living structures that support the defacing of the *Imago Dei* in all human beings. I know that this is hard work. It is easier to simply rinse and repeat after race, its prejudices, and stereotypes than to act on what we say we believe as Christians and to act out our baptismal identity. But, for those who are "dead with Christ," we rise to transcend all categories. Because it is not enough to say that Jesus' good news is raceless.

No, you and I must do the work of demonstrating it by stepping out of and refusing to put cultural groups into the boxes that race comes in. This work begins with us who continue to segregate on Sunday mornings. We color in the face of God and frame our decision to break the second commandment in our sanctuaries. We said that the social-coloring of skin was indicative of Christlikeness. We prop race up theologically and deny our baptismal identity to pick up the privileges of whiteness.

We racialized Jesus' gospel, so we must question both the reasoning and race faithfully until we have absolutely no faith in race. We must tear down the idols we have made to ourselves and defy this 400-year-old lie. Let's find and feature our deepest communal meanings as members of Christ's body.

People of faith and no faith at all are faced with this four-letter word that curses any attempt at building healthy and faithful communities. Because race wasn't created to reconcile us to each other, to bring about justice, equality, or unity. It has no biological basis and sits on a pseudo-theological foundation. So, let's practice a faith that is raceless by deracializing our images of the Divine Community, questioning the role of race in human being and belonging and decentering race in spiritual formation as a practice of discipleship for a "kin-dom" coming.

This is not a call to action but an action plan. Followers of Jesus know exactly where he is going, as all roads lead to Calvary. In turn, we must die to the self that is racialized. What follows then is our witness, our work, and our covenant.

Our Witness

We believe that the gospel of Jesus is raceless, that Jesus lived as a Jewish man and should not be exorcised from his cultural setting in Nazareth, an agricultural community, to serve the needs of American culture, its stereotypes, and prejudices.

We believe that no Person of the Trinity is a member of a racialized group, as race is not eternal and consequently the divine will and work does not endorse or support the social privileges, perks, micro-aggressions, and macro-oppressions of the sociopolitical construct of race.

We believe human beings were not created to be color-coded, that all bodies are created equal—not for competition and without comparison.

We believe that our allegiance to a racial group directly conflicts with our baptismal identity.

We stand in agreement with the words of Paul as recorded in his letter to the church at Galatia: "As many of you as were baptized into Christ have clothed yourselves with Christ. There is no longer Jew or Greek, there is no longer slave or free, there is no longer male or female; for all of you are one in Christ Jesus" (Gal. 3:27-28).

Denying race as a source of identity works to unite us more fully with Jesus and the global community, while race prevents his reconciling work, dividing us while depriving us of our full and authentic selves. Denying race as a category for human grouping challenges the self-imposed boundaries enforced by stereotypes and prejudices. Rejecting the authority of race, we believe that the body of Christ is not segregated—just as the members of our physical body cannot be separated. The raceless gospel is evidence of our baptismal identity, our new human being, belonging, and community with, in, and through Jesus (Gal. 3:27-28) We strive, therefore, to practice a faith that seeks understanding without race and to live as next of kin to all human beings in support of the "kin-dom" that is coming.

Our Work

Study race as a spiritual discipline. What do you believe about race? How does your faith call you to respond to race and its progeny?

Examine race. What does race look like in your life and in the lives of those closest to you? Place its stereotypes and prejudices alongside your religious or moral convictions.

Ask questions about race and map its relationship to you. How did you come to know race and to be known by a racialized identity (beige, black, brown, red, yellow, or white)?

Talk about race and what it means to you. Tell the story of your relationship with race.

Challenge the position of race in your life and the way it positions you in community. It is a social arrangement. You don't have to accept the terms and conditions of this agreement.

Form friendships across cultures. This kind of relationship can change the power dynamics of race and the ways in which we relate to each other.

Resolve to live a raceless life. Stop coloring Jesus in and framing the divine in your homes and sanctuaries. You are willfully and artistically breaking the second commandment (Exod. 20:4). Also, give up coloring people in. Let genuine relationships inspire you to live, love, and serve outside of "the color line."

Our Covenant

As the children of God, we do hereby covenant with God, ourselves, and our neighbors to not employ the historical and personal lens of race or its social truths in the interpretation of scripture, in our understanding of the will of God, the work of the Holy Spirit, or the ministry of Jesus Christ to deny the preservation of a racialized worldview.

We agree not to speak of race as having divine power or as a member of the Holy Community but as a social construct and a social contract that we no longer agree to.

We agree not to recreate the Holy Community in the images of race.

We will not amend, modify, or alter the attributes of the Holy Community to suit the causes of race.

We will not subject God or God's will to the social truths and purposes of race.

We will regularly examine our thoughts, speech, behavior and relationships as they concern race and the practice of our faith with God, ourselves, and our neighbors

We will be intentional in our awareness of race worship and available to question the rationale behind our continued observance of race's commandments and our belief in its social parables.

We commit to courageous truth-telling about our existence and experiences without employing the lens of race or the leverage of white supremacy.

We will work to redefine our lives, faith/beliefs, relationships, vocation/ work, experiences, habits/hobbies/interests, and all the members of our bodies apart from the social prescriptions, cultural expectations, historical vocabulary, and definitions of race.

We will denounce our social, cultural, familial, emotional, theological, and religious allegiance to race in order that we might experience a truer and deeper freedom in relationship with God, ourselves and our neighbors.

We will not assign human worth and potential, attribute social success or failure, assume educational background or vocational pursuits, guilt or innocence, personal threat or safety to the social-coloring of a person's skin or any other physical attribute.

We will not repeat the curses of race or pass down its traditions of prejudice and stereotyping, supremacy, and powerlessness to our children and likewise not accept the privileges, perks, and special benefits of whiteness or pass down the lens that allows us to look away or to blatantly ignore those experiencing poverty, marginalization, minoritization, and oppression because they are not socially-colored white.

We will love our God, ourselves, and our neighbors apart from the conditions and without the assistance of race.

I am building a raceless world as practice for the "kin-dom" that is coming. And if you are wondering how you can do it, then let this book serve as a building permit. I don't need to sign it for you to get to work. You have your instructions and the only measurement you'll ever need: "I am somebody." So, let's get started.

It will require some heavy lifting. Raise your hands. I want to see both hands. Show me all ten fingers. Do you want to be saved from race, delivered from the body of this social death? Then say it: "I am somebody."

This is rebirth and our new beginning: to know ourselves as made in the uncategorical image of our Creator and to live undivided lives that are in touch with everyone. The old way and its many divisions are what we must be stripped of. And how massive and all-meaningful then is Christ's body! The knowing is so vast that it is still occurring. This baptismal identity was never meant to be paired with or piled onto another way of being. No, all those categories and social positions should float to the top of the water during baptism. Dead in the water or if that is too dramatic, those labels are slippery when wet.

Now identified with Christ as siblings and citizens of a new "kin-dom" that is coming, baptism then is the entryway. The re-enactment of Jesus' death, burial, and resurrection is not simply a new lease on life.[12] We decrease, and Jesus increases in us.[13] We go down, and he comes up— but not just in conversation. We become an extension of Christ's body. In Christ, we all fit right in while entering our true selves more deeply.

Segregated churches resulting in Christ's dismembered body, North American Christians have been disconnected for far too long. In *Luminous Darkness: A Personal Interpretation of the Anatomy of Segregation and the Ground of Hope*, Howard Thurman puts it this way: "If a black Christian and a white Christian, in encounter, cannot reach out to each other in mutual realization because of that which they are experiencing in common, then there should be no surprise that the Christian institution has been powerless in the presence of the color bar in society. Rather it has reflected the presence of the color bar within its own institutional life."[3]23

This is not a reflection of baptismal identity, but it is what people see when they look at the North American church. As a result, it must be taken back to the water. Hold your nose and go down, church. I baptize you now in the raceless gospel of Jesus Christ. Amen.

Appendix

"Take Me to the Water":
A Baptismal Liturgy

As many of you as were baptized with Christ have clothed yourselves with Christ. There is no longer Jew or Greek, there is no longer slave or free, there is no longer male and female; for all of you are one in Christ Jesus (Gal. 3:27-28.).

The Elements
The Ritual of Baptism
A Centering Prayer
Scripture Readings
"Take me to the water"
Call and Response
Communal Reading
Prayer of Blessing
A Closing Prayer

About the Liturgy
Before the "Four Spiritual Laws" or the "Roman Road" to salvation, there was baptism. "Take Me to the Water" is a resource for churches that do not view baptism as a dunking contest but want to live out the ritual's meanings in deep and abiding ways. Following Jesus' lead, his disciples enter the water as a sign of their commitment to his life and teachings (Luke 3:31-32). A symbol of their own death, burial, and resurrection, baptism has been described as a "watery grave." Titus says baptizands are saved through the water (3:5). Believers come out on the other side with a new life in and through Jesus the Christ.

Womb water, a mysterious entrance and exit strategy, Paul explains to the believers in Rome: "Do you not know that all of us who have been baptized into Christ Jesus were baptized into his death? Therefore, we have been buried with him by baptism into death, so that, just as Christ was raised from the dead by the glory of the Father, so we too might walk in the newness of life" (Rom. 6:3-4). During baptism, we enter the water and into Christ's body. Now connected with other believers, we become members of one another—not a building.

Water and the Spirit hovering, baptism is our new creation narrative and in Christ we "live, move, and have (our) being." Baptism must have rippling effects on our lives; if it does not, then, take me to the water.

The Ritual of Baptism

Jesus asks John to take him to the water (Matt. 3:13-17). The convert's baptism is one of the first steps, evidence of beginning one's walk with Jesus. We follow him there. We take on the water and its meanings: death, burial, and resurrection.

Through the waters of baptism, we are reborn as new creatures in Christ Jesus, as members of his body and of one another. Through the water and in the Spirit, baptism is the convert's new beginning. Baptism is the starting point of one's relationship with Jesus, a reminder that we are led by the Spirit as God's beloved.

Siblings in Christ, baptism—the witness of water and the Holy Spirit— is not a good scrub but "the cleansing flood." Water rising above our heads, this ritual of baptism renders us dead to one life and alive to the next. Citizens of an undivided "kin-dom" that is coming, we are taken to the water. The portal of new life in Jesus the Christ, our Savior, we take from the waters an uncategorical way of being and only faint memories of who we once were, never to be heard from again. We are called by a new name and are identified by, in, and through Christ's body only.

A Centering Prayer

Christ-followers, who claim his body as our own, bring us together some way, somehow. Because that four-letter word has cursed us to our core and to our corners of the world.

Forgive us for segregating the sacred, for coloring in your face, for scratching out the Imago Dei in certain human beings, for loving prejudicially, for practicing mercy selectively, for walking away from the marginalized and minoritized—rather than walking humbly.

Give us the courage to dive into why the waters of baptism have not troubled the caste system with a good paint job that is race. Give us "faith seeking understanding" without it.

In the name of the one who stood in line and was baptized as a demonstration of new life, Jesus the Christ, in whose name we gather and behind whom we fall in line, I pray. Amen.

Scripture Readings

Then Jesus came from Galilee to John at the Jordan, to be baptized by him. John would have prevented him saying, "I need to be baptized by you, and do you come to me?" But Jesus answered him, "Let it be so for now; for it is proper for us in this way to fulfill all righteousness." Then he consented. And when Jesus had been baptized, just as he came up from the water, suddenly the heavens were opened up to him and he saw the Spirit of God descending like a dove and alighting on him. And a voice from heaven said, "This is my Son, the Beloved, with whom I am well pleased." (Matt. 3:13-17)

Jesus answered, "Very truly, I tell you, no one can see the kingdom of God without being born of water and Spirit." (John 3:5)

Peter said to them, "Repent and be baptized every one of you in the name of Jesus Christ so that your sins may be forgiven; and you will receive the gift of the Holy Spirit. For the promise is for you, for your children, and for all who are far away, everyone whom the Lord our God calls to him." (Acts 2:38-39)

For just as the body is one and has many members, and all the members of the body, though many, are one body, so it is with Christ. For in the one Spirit, we were all baptized into one body—Jews or Greeks, slaves or free— and we were made to drink of one Spirit. (1 Cor. 12:12-13)

"Take me to the water"

Take me to the water,   In the name of Jesus,
Take me to the water,   In the name of Jesus,
Take me to the water,   In the name of Jesus,
     To be baptized.   We shall be saved.

None but the righteous,   I know I got religion,
None but the righteous,   I know I got religion,
None but the righteous,   I know I got religion,
     Shall see God.   Yes, I do.

I love Jesus,   Glory, hallelujah,
I love Jesus,   Glory, hallelujah,
I love Jesus,   Glory, hallelujah,
     Yes, I do.   To be baptized.

Call and Response

Do you renounce the dehumanizing spirit of this world, refuse to support the structures that aim to break the human soul and our ties to each other as image-bearers of God?

I do.

Do you reject the notion that you must assimilate to a culture or pledge allegiance to a country to experience God's saving grace, mercy, and love?

I do.

Do you repent of your sins and turn away from all wickedness, which thwarts your transformation as a new creature in Christ Jesus?

I do.

Do you accept the kinship as one of God's children, the fellowship as a member of Christ's body and the tutorship as a habitation of the Holy Spirit?

I do.

Do you accept Jesus as your Lord and Savior, teacher and friend, go-to guide and travel companion?

I do.

Communal Reading

Galatians 3:27-28 contains what many scholars believe to be the church's first creed, its first confession of belief—not about God or even Jesus but who they are in the Spirit. "It is through baptism that these distinctions are exposed as false," writes Stephen J. Patterson in *The Forgotten Creed: Christianity's Original Struggle Against Bigotry, Slavery, and Sexism* (Oxford University Press, 2018, p. 24). Undermining the power dynamics of culture, class and gender, the early church was unified in decentering power.

Let us read this confession together: For you are the children of God in the Spirit. There is no Jew or Greek, there is no slave or free, there is no male and female; for you are all one in the Spirit.

Prayer of Blessing

Baptism was of primary importance to Jesus' ministry and is the universal sign of a Christian. It is subversion by immersion, undermining the systems and structures that once held power over the new believer as one goes under. This is not a religious habit, merely our obedience to the way Jesus did it. But it is the way of Jesus, evidence that we are following in his footsteps. Consequently, a certificate of baptism is not evidence of a finished work and should not be treated as a blue ribbon for righteousness. No, we Christians die daily (1 Cor. 15:31). Our former selves were not meant to survive.

Hands laid in prayer are aids in this self-mortification.

For the baptizand: By the grace of God and upon the profession of your faith, I baptize you in the name of Jesus the Christ. May all the world's labels float to the top. May all that hindered the work of the Holy Spirit in this flesh be dead in the water. Born of water and of Spirit, may you rise with new life and vigor. Amen.

(After the baptism, invite members to welcome the new convert with the following words.)

For fellow baptized believers: Through baptism, you are joined to the body of Christ and to his members, who welcome you with joy and thanksgiving into God's re-creating work and witness in us and in the world.

A Closing Prayer

God of bodies watered down, diluted by divisions, polluted by race and its progeny, gather us now.

Christ-followers, who claim his body as our own, bring us together some way, somehow. Because that four-letter word has cursed us to our core and to our corners of the world.

Forgive us for segregating the sacred, for coloring in your face, for scratching out the Imago Dei in certain human beings, for loving prejudicially, for practicing mercy selectively, for walking away from the marginalized and minoritized—rather than walking humbly.

Give us the courage to dive into why the waters of baptism have not troubled the caste system with a good paint job that is race. Give us "faith seeking understanding" without it.

In the name of the one who stood in line and was baptized as a demonstration of new life, Jesus the Christ, in whose name we gather and behind whom we fall in line, I pray. Amen.

NOTES

1 Howard Thurman, *The Search for Common Ground* (Richmond, IN: Friends United Press, 1986), xiii.

2 Rom. 6:4.

3 John 3:30.

4 Titus 3:5.

5 John 3:5, *MSG*.

6 Matt. 4:19.

7 Matt. 11:29.

8 Matt. 16:24.

9 1 Sam. 3:1.

10 Thomas G. Long, *Testimony: Talking Ourselves into Being Christian* (San Francisco: Jossey-Bass, 2004), 6.

11 Ibid., 11.

12 John 3:5.

13 Titus 3:5, John 3:3.

14 Rom. 6:4, Col. 2:12.

15 Acts 2:38. See also Mark 16:16.

16 Dietrich Bonhoeffer, *Life Together* (New York: Harper & Brothers Publishers, 1954), 21.

17 2 Cor. 5:16-17a.

18 Howard Thurman, *Jesus and the Disinherited* (Boston: Beacon Press, 1976), xix.

19 Michael Omi and Howard Winant, *Racial Formation in the United States: From the 1960s to the 1990s* (New York: Routledge, 1994), 55.

20 Philip Neri, "Baptism and the Manumission of Negro Slaves in the Early Colonial Period," *Records of the American Catholic Historical Society of Philadelphia* 51, no. 3/4 (1940): 220–32, http://www.jstor.org/stable/44209369.

21 William H. Willimon, *Peculiar Speech: Preaching to the Baptized* (Grand Rapids: William B. Eerdmans Publishing Co., 1992), 7.

22 Howard Thurman: *The Creative Encounter: An Interpretation of Religion and the Social Witness* (Richmond, IN: Friends United Press, 1954), 19.

23 "For every (person), there is a necessity to establish as securely as possible the lines along which (one) proposes to live (one's) life. In developing (your) life's working paper, (you) must take into account many factors, in (your) reaction to which (you) may seem to throw them out of line with their true significance." Howard Thurman, *Deep is the Hunger* (1951, repr., Richmond, IN: Friends United Press, 2000), 64.

24 This is a nod to *Samuel Proctor: My Moral Odyssey* (King of Prussia, PA: Judson Press, 1989).

25 Henry Louis Gates Jr., *Loose Canons: Notes on the Culture Wars* (New York: Oxford University Press, Inc., 1992), 50.

26 "For in one Spirit we were all baptized into one body—Jews or Greeks, slave or free—and we were all made to drink of one Spirit" (1 Cor. 12:13).

27 "The sociologist John Dollard's quaint references to 'our temporary Negroes' and the history of Barry Goldberg's discussions of 'not-yet white' immigrants are striking examples. Other labels, such as 'situationally white,' 'not quite white,' 'off-white,' 'semi-racialized,' and 'conditionally white,' convey the ambiguity and uncertainty of an immigrant racial status that was constantly under review." David R. Roediger, *Working Toward Whiteness: How America's Immigrants Became White* (Cambridge, MA: Basic Books, 2005), 13.

28 Nikole Hannah-Jones, Caitlin Roper, Ilena Silverman, and Jake Silverstein, *The 1619 Project: A New Origin Story* (New York: One World, 2021). The poem appears just before the preface of the book.

29 Ibid., xxv.

30 Ibid.

31 Katherine Gerber, *Christian Slavery: Conversion and Race in the Protestant Atlantic World* (Philadelphia: University of Pennsylvania Press, 2018), 14.

32 It is often referred to as the "Transatlantic slave trade," but the water is not guilty of trafficking humans.

33 Equiano Olaudah, *The Interesting Narrative of the Life of Equiano Olaudah, or Gustavus Vassa, the African, Written by Himself,* in *The Norton Anthology of African American Literature,* Henry Louis Gates Jr. and Nellie Y. McKay, gen. eds. (New York: W.W. Norton & Co., Inc., 1997), 155.

34 Ibid., 148.

35 Ibid., 157.

36 Orlando Patterson, *Slavery and Social Death: A Comparative Study with a New Preface* (Cambridge, MA: Harvard University Press, 2018), 71.

37 A noteworthy aside: Found in the special collections library of England's Bristol University by history professor Marcus Rediker, titled "The Petition of the Sharks of Africa" and addressed to "To the Right Honourable the Lords Spiritual and Temporal of Great Britain, in Parliament assembled," the letter is satirical, and the writer versed in dark humor. The writer asked the recipients not to end the slave trade, as it provided an unparalleled meal plan for the marine fish. Different from the traditional images and stories of abolition, it should be remembered in our storytelling, nonetheless. Marcus Rediker, "Slavery: A Shark's Perspective: A strange text sheds new light on the true roots of abolition," http://archive.boston.com/news/globe/ideas/articles/2007/09/23/slavery_a_sharks_perspective/, Sept. 23, 2007.

38 A belief of medieval Christianity in a hierarchical structure for all living things, which was commanded by God.

39 Albert J. Raboteau, *Slave Religion: The "Invisible Institution" in the Antebellum South* (New York: Oxford University Press, 1978), 98.

40 "Enslaved people also used Christianity in the courts to gain their freedom, when, presumably careful negotiation with their masters and a network of kin and contacts had failed them. In 1644, a mulatto slave named Manuel sued successfully before the Virginia Assembly in Jamestown to be 'adjudged no Slave but to serve as other Christian Servants do.' Manuel made an explicit connection between his Christianity and his right to serve a lesser term as an indentured servant, not as a slave for life." Gerber, *Christian Slavery*, 102.

41 Albert J. Raboteau, *Canaan Land: A Religious History of African Americans* (New York: Oxford University Press, 2001), 16.

42 Leonard L. Haynes Jr., *The Negro Community Within American Protestantism, 1619–1844* (Boston: Christopher Publishing House, 1953), 32-33.

43 Michael O. Emerson and Christian Smith, *Divided by Faith: Evangelical Religion and the Problem of Race in America* (New York: Oxford University Press, 2000), 24.

44 M. Shawn Copeland, *Enfleshing Freedom: Body, Race, and Being* (Minneapolis: Fortress Press, 2010), 24.

45 John W. Blassingame, ed., *Slave Testimony: Two Centuries of Letters, Speeches, Interviews, and Autobiographies* (Baton Rouge: Louisiana State University Press, 1977), 276.

46 Ibid., 276.

47 Jemar Tisby, *The Color of Compromise: The Truth About the American Church's Complicity in Racism* (Grand Rapids: Zondervan, 2019), 26.

48 Rom. 6:15-23.

49 1 Pet. 2:18-25.

50 Anne H. Pinn and Anthony B. Pinn, *Fortress Introduction to Black Church History* (Minneapolis: Fortress Press, 2002), 4.

51 William D. Philips, *Slavery from Roman Times to the Early Transatlantic Slave Trade* (Minneapolis: University of Minnesota Press, 1985), 35.

52 Winthrop Jordan, *The White Man's Burden: Historical Origins of Racism in the United States* (New York: Oxford University Press, 1974), 51.

53 I coined the term social-coloring to capture the fact that there are no physically colored beige (mixed race), black, brown, red, yellow, or black people. Race is a social arrangement and a social agreement to see each other using these arbitrary colors.

54 Matt. 20:20-28, 24:36-51.

55 Eph. 2:1-10.

56 Tisby, *The Color of Compromise*, 39.

57 "Prior to 1640, there is very little evidence to show how Negroes were treated. After 1640, there is mounting evidence that some Negroes were in fact being treated as slaves. This is to say that the twin essences of slavery—lifetime service and inherited status—first became evident during the twenty years prior to the beginning of legal formation. After 1660, slavery was written into statute law" (p. 40). "After 1640, when surviving Virginia county court records began to mention Negroes, sales for life, often including any future progeny, were recorded in unmistakable language" (p. 42). Jordan, *The White Man's Burden*.

58 This is a misnomer. Winthrop Jordan writes, "The terms Indian and Negro were both borrowed from the Hispanic languages, the one originally deriving from (mistaken) geographic locality and the other from human complexion" (p. 52).

59 Rebecca Anne Goetz, *The Baptism of Early Virginia: How Christianity Created Race* (Baltimore: Johns Hopkins University Press, 2012), 2.

60 Susan Juster and Lisa MacFarlane, eds., *A Mighty Baptism: Race, Gender, and the Creation of American Protestantism* (Ithaca, NY: Cornell University Press, 1996), 14.

61 Gerber, *Christian Slavery*, 2.

62 Jordan, *The White Man's Burden*, 52.

63 Gerber, *Christian Slavery*, 74.

64 Ibid., 89.

65 Frank M. Snowden Jr., *Before Color Prejudice: The Ancient View of Blacks* (Cambridge, MA: Harvard University, 2983), 63.

66 Cain Hope Felder, *Troubling the Biblical Waters: Race, Class, and Family* (1990, repr., Maryknoll, NY: Orbis Books, 1993), 3.

67 Jamelle Bouie, "The Dark Side of the Enlightenment: How the Enlightenment created modern race thinking, and why we should confront it," June 5, 2018, https://slate.com/news-and-politics/2018/06/taking-the-enlightenment-seriously-requires-talking-about-race.html, Accessed on February 22, 2022.

68 As quoted in Jamelle Bouie's essay above.

69 Michael Omi and Howard Winant, *Racial Formation in the United States: From the 1960s to the 1990s* (New York: Routledge, 1994), 55.

70 Thomas Gossett, *Race: The History of An Idea in America* (New York: Oxford University Press, 1997), 39.

71 "AAA Statement on Race," May 17, 1998, https://www.americananthro.org/ConnectWithAAA/Content aspx?ItemNumber=2583.

72 Toni Morrison, *Playing in the Dark: Whiteness and the Literary Imagination* (New York: Vintage Books, 1992), 63.

73 Isabel Wilkerson, *Caste: The Origins of Our Discontents* (New York: Random House, 2020), 17.

74 Exod. 20:2. See also James Baldwin's "Notes on the House of Bondage," https://www.thenation.com/article/archive/notes-house-bondage/, Nov. 1, 1980.

75 Charles W. Mills, The Racial Contract (Ithaca, NY: Cornell University, 1997), 3.

76 Ian Haney Lopez, *White by Law: The Legal Construction of Race, Revised and Updated* (New York: New York University Press, 2006), xv.

77 David R. Roediger, *Working Towards Whiteness: How America's Immigrants Became White* (New York: Basic Books, 2005), 14-15.

78 James Baldwin, "White Man's Guilt," in *Black on White: Black Writers on What It Means to Be White,* David R. Roediger, ed. (New York: Schocken Books, 1998), 323.

79 Brian Bantum, *The Death of Race: Building a New Christianity in a Racial World* (Minneapolis: Fortress Press, 2016), 14.

80 Some European colonizers believed that African people did not have a soul.

81 See W.E.B. DuBois, *The Souls of Black Folk* (New York: Penguin Books, 1989), for the meaning of double-consciousness.

82 Frederick Douglass, *Narrative of the Life of Frederick Douglass,* in *The Classic Slave Narratives,* Henry Louis Gates, ed. (New York: A Mentor Book, 1987), 326.

83 Dwight N. Hopkins, *Down, Up, and Over: Slave Religion and Black Theology* (Minneapolis: Fortress Press, 2000), 15.

84 Raboteau, *Slave Religion,* 121.

85 For more on this practice, see Charles Colcock Jones' *The Religious Instruction of the Negroes in the United States,* published in 1842.

86 General Assembly, *Acts passed at a General Assembly of the Commonwealth of Virginia* (Richmond: [s.n.], 1831), 107-108. See also https://encyclopediavirginia.org/entries/an-act-to-amend-the-act-concerning-slaves-free-negroes-and-mulattoes-april-7-1831/

87 Raboteau, *Slave Religion,* 122.

88 Ibid., 123.

89 Raboteau, *Canaan Land,* 44.

90 Ibid., 17.

91 Ibid., 19.

92 Melville Herskovits, *The Myth of the Negro Past* (Boston: Beacon Press, 1958), 220-221.

93 In one case, the members were known as the "Supervising Committee" (see p. 47).

94 Raboteau, *Canaan Land,* 14.

95 Mechal Sobel, *Trabelin' On: The Slave Journey to an Afro-Baptist Faith* (Westport, CT: Greenwood Press, 1979), 205.

96 Henry H. Mitchell, *Black Church Beginnings: The Long-Hidden Realities of the First Years* (Grand Rapids: William B. Eerdmans Publishing Co., 2004), 49.

97 Ibid., 51.

98 Raboteau, *Canaan Land,* 24.

99 Note: In 1838, the Virginia legislature refused to grant any "black church" independence. Mitchell, *Black Church Beginnings,* 48.

100 Pinn, *Fortress Introduction to Black Church History,* vii.

101 Howard Thurman, *Luminous Darkness: A Personal Interpretation of the Anatomy of Segregation and the Ground of Hope* (Richmond, IN: Friends United Press, 1989), 21.

102 Joseph Washington, "How Black is Black Religion?" in *Quest for a Black Theology*, James J. Gardiner and J. Deotis Roberts, eds. (Philadelphia: Pilgrim Press, 1971), 28.

103 Stephen R. Haynes, *The Last Segregated Hour: The Memphis Kneel-Ins and the Campaign for Southern Church Desegregation* (New York: Oxford University Press, 2012), 3. This book covers the church desegregation campaign that occurred in the South from 1960–1965.

104 Ibid., 5.

105 The National Congregations study is the work of Duke University and its director, Mark Chaves. The data can be found at https://sites.duke.edu/ncsweb/explore-the-data/ and under congregational quick stats followed by the subcategory "membership" and then "Percent White."

106 Michael Lipka, "Many U.S. Congregations are Still Racially Segregated but Things are Changing," http://www.pewresearch.org/fact-tank/2014/12/08/many-u-s-congregations-are-still-racially-segregated-but-things-are-changing-2/, Pew Research Center, Dec. 8, 2014.

107 Thurman, *Luminous Darkness*, 6.

108 Ibid., 17.

109 Ibid., 18.

110 Ibid., 5.

111 "Most often, the races are named by colors: white, yellow, black, red and brown. It was (Johann Friedrich) Blumenbach who coined the word Caucasian to describe the white race. It is curious that this word—which is still widely used—is based upon a single skull in Blumenbach's collection, which came from the Caucasian mountain region of Russia." Thomas F. Gossett, *Race: The History of an Idea in America* (New York: Oxford University Press, 1997), 38.

112 Toni Morrison, *The Origin of Others* (Cambridge, MA: Harvard University Press, 2017), 20.

113 Thurman, *Luminous Darkness*, 6.

114 James Baldwin, *The Cross of Redemption: Uncollected Writings* (New York: Pantheon Books, 2010), 73.

115 Ibid., 95.

116 Martin Luther King Jr., "The Role of the Church in Facing the Nation's Chief Moral Dilemma," Conference on Christian Faith and Human Relations, Nashville, TN, April 25,1957.http://okra.stanford.edu/transcription/document_images/Vol04Scans/184_1957The%20Role%20of%20the%20Church.pdf, Accessed on Feb. 19, 2022.

117 "Kin-dom" is a word coined by Franciscan nun Georgene Wilson and is often used to replace kingdom, which has patriarchal and exclusively masculine implications.

118 Heb. 13:8.

119 Mark 4:38.

120 Mark 4:41.

121 John 11:7-8.

122 Mark 6:4.

123 Mark 6:5, *MSG*.

124 John 11:43.

125 John 11:25.

126 William Willimon, *Why Jesus?* (Nashville: Abingdon Press, 2010), 126.

127 1 Cor. 12:5-6, 8.

128 1 Cor. 12:12.

129 1 Cor. 12:13.

130 John 7:38, *MSG*.

131 Matt. 16:24.

132"Baptism," William Willimon, https://thevalueofsparrows.com/2015/11/16/baptism-repent-by-william-willimon/.

133 Mark 1:4.

134 It is a play on my version of Willimon's words: "Repent, change your ways, and get washed."

135 1 Cor. 12:13.

136 Mark 10:39.

137 Raymond E. Brown, *An Introduction to the New Testament* (New York: Doubleday, 1997), 279.

138 Acts 2:38-39.

139 Act 8:6-7.

140 Acts 8:12-13.

141 Acts 9:4.

142 Acts 9:15-16.

143 Acts 9:17-18.

144 Brown, *An Introduction to the New Testament*, 422.

145 Walter Brueggemann, *A Way Other Than Our Own: Devotions for Lent* (Louisville, KY: Westminster John Knox Press, 2017), 18.

146 N.T. Wright, *Paul: A Biography* (New York: HarperCollins Publishers, 2018), 5.

147 Willimon, *Why Jesus?* 78.

148 William Willimon, *The Intrusive Word: Preaching to the Unbaptized* (Grand Rapids: William B. Eerdmans Publishing Co., 1994), 6.

149 James Baldwin, "The Price May Be Too High," *The New York Times*, Feb. 2, 1969.

150 Robert P. Jones, *White Too Long: The Legacy of White Supremacy in American Christianity* (New York: Simon & Schuster, 2020), 5-6.

151 The white savior complex impacts persons who, due to their sense of social superiority, feel called to save other ethnic groups or nationalities—often without their permission, input as to the support needed, and/or interest in the impact of an unwarranted intervention. To learn more, read: Teju Cole, "The White-Savior Industrial Complex, *The Atlantic*, March 21, 2012.

152 Edward J. Blum and Paul Harvey, *The Color of Christ: The Son of God and the Saga of Race in America* (Chapel Hill: The University of North Carolina Press, 2012), 9,10.

153 See Kelly Brown Douglas, *The Black Christ* (1994, repr., Maryknoll, NY: Orbis Books, 2002).

154 William R. Jones, *Is God a White Racist? A Preamble to Black Theology* (Boston: Beacon Press, 1998), 3.

155 See James H. Cone, *God of the Oppressed* (1975, repr., Maryknoll, NY: Orbis Books, 1999).

156 Jones, *Is God a White Racist?*, 5.

157 1 Cor. 12:13.

158 Sandra M. Schneiders, "Scripture and Spirituality," in *Christian Spirituality: Origins to the Twelfth Century*, Bernard McGinn, John Meyendorff, and Jean Leclercq, eds. (New York: The Crossroad Publishing Co., 1992), 5.

159 William Waller Hening, ed., *The Statutes at Large; Being a Collection of All the Laws of Virginia from the First Session of the Legislature, in the Year 1619* (New York: R.&W.& G. Bartow, 1823), 2:260.

160 John 3:3.

161 This purification is evidenced in Titus 3:5: "he saved us, not because of any works of righteousness that we had done, but according to his mercy, through the water of rebirth and renewal by the Holy Spirit."

162 Thurman, *The Search for Common Ground*, 78.

163 Matt. 3:13-17.

164 Matt. 3:15.

165 Exod. 12:26-26.

166 Exod. 40:12-15; Lev. 16:26-28, 17:15; Num. 8:5-7.

167 Everett Ferguson, *Baptism in the Early Church: History, Theology, and Liturgy in the First Five Centuries* (Grand Rapids: William B. Eerdmans Publishing Co., 2009), 36.

168 Acts 10:47.

169 Acts 8:26-40.

170 This is a quote from the *Demonstration*, translated by Joseph P. Smith, *St. Irenaeus: Proof of the Apostolic Preaching*, Ancient Christian Writers 16 (New York: Newman [Paulist], 1952), 49.

171 "The flesh is not, according to Marcion, immersed [tinguitur] unless it be in virginity, widowhood, or celibacy, or has purchased baptism by divorce" (Against Marcion). Ibid., 277.

172 Ibid., 280.

173 Ibid., 301.

174 Tertullian, *On Baptism*, 1.2-3.

175 Ibid., 401.

176 Ibid., 547-548.

177 Athanasius, *Discourses Against Arians*, 2.18.41. Ibid., 456.

178 Athanasius, Letter 49 [To Dracontius], 4. Ibid., 455.

179 Ibid., 466.

180 Ibid., 468.

181 "Emergency baptism of children had begun at the latest by 200 and after Tertullian we do not hear of opposition to infant baptism. However, if children were healthy, there is no evidence that their parents presented them for baptism. The instruction to parents to baptize their children begins in the late fourth century, and the routine baptism of babies belongs to the fifth century and after, when evidence for accommodations of the baptism ceremony to the presence of infant begins to appear."

182 John 3:5.

183 2 Cor. 5:16-17.

184 Elisabeth Schussler Fiorenza, "Paul and the Politics of Interpretation," in *Paul and Politics: Ekklesia, Israel, Imperium, Interpretation*, Richard A. Horsley, ed. (Harrisburg, PA: Trinity Press International, 2000), 45.

185 1 Cor. 12:13.

186 Col. 2:11-12.

187 1 Cor. 12:12-27 positions the Christian believer who, as a member of the body, cannot reject another member because it does not have the same function or features.

188 Mark 10:39.

189 Matt. 16:24.

190 Gal. 3:27-28.

191 "But again, Paul did not compose the creed. He borrowed it and in so doing, he changed it, adapted it." Stephen J. Patterson, *The Forgotten Creed: Christianity's Original Struggle Against Bigotry, Slavery, & Sexism* (New York: Oxford University Press, 2018), 5-6.

192 Ibid., 4.

193 Ibid., 6.

194 Phil. 2:7.

195 Patterson, *The Forgotten Creed*, 6.

196 Ibid., 3.

197 Col. 3:5,

198 Col. 3:10-11.

199 Acts 11:16.

200 Stanley J. Grenz, *Theology for the Community of God* (Grand Rapids: William B. Eerdmans Publishing Co., 1994), 427.

201 Howard Thurman surmised, "Life is against all dualism, life is one. ... Always, against all that fragments and shatters, and against all things that separate and divide within and without, life labors to meld together into a single harmony." Thurman, *The Search for Common Ground*, x.

202 1 Cor. 15:39.

203 Thomas Gossett, *Race: The History of an Idea in America* (New York; Oxford University Press, 1997), 36, 37.

204 James K. Perkinson, *White Theology: Outing White Supremacy in Modernity* (New York: Palgrave Macmillan, 2004), 239, 240.

205 Matt. 16:18.

206 Acts 2:46.

207 This is a nod to the song "This is America" by Donald Glover.

208 Gal. 1:8.

209 This word is attributed to a Franciscan nun named Georgene Wilson.

210 John 3:1-21.

211 Eph. 1:22-23.

212 Rom. 9:1-5.

213 Matt. 1:22, 2:15, 2:23, 4:14, 8:17, 12:17, 13:35, 21:4, 26:56, 27:35.

214 Jesus has also been re-created as African American, Asian, Indian, and Indigenous in response to the socially-colored white Jesus.

215 Stephen Prothero, *American Jesus: How the Son of God Became a National Icon* (New York: Farrar, Straus, and Giroux, 2003), 157.

216 Matt. 11:15.

217 This does not suggest that the Black Power and Red Power movements, which sought the freedom of self-determination for the First Nation people and the expression of pride in one's heritage while calling for economic empowerment for African Americans, were not necessary. The point here is to decenter whiteness and to remove its supervisory capacity, its position in the decision-making, approving, and determining of human worth, dignity, being, and belonging.

218 In Luke 20:1-8, the chief priests question Jesus' authority. In turn, Jesus questions the authority of baptism, whether it is from heaven or manufactured by human hands.

219 C. Eric Lincoln, *Coming Through the Fire: Surviving Race and Place in America* (Durham, NC: Duke University Press, 1996), 94.

220 N.T. Wright, *Following Jesus: Biblical Reflections on Discipleship* (Grand Rapids: William B. Eerdmans Publishing Co., 1994), xiv.

221 Howard Thurman, *The Inward Journey* (Richmond, IN: Friends United Press, 1961), 40.

222 Gen. 2:7.

223 Forrest E. Harris Sr., ed., *What Does It Mean to Be Black and Christian? The Survival of a Whole People: The Meaning of the African American Church* (Nashville: Townsend Press, 1998).

224 This is an excerpt from Howard Thurman's baccalaureate address at Spelman College, delivered on May 4, 1980. Jo Moore Stewart, ed., *The Spelman Messenger*, vol. 96, no. 4 (Summer 1980), 14-15.

225 David E. Fitch, *The Church of Us vs. Them: Freedom from a Faith That Feeds on Making Enemies* (Grand Rapids: Brazos Press, 2019), 8.

226 Eph. 2:14-16.

227 2 Cor. 5:17.

228 2 Cor. 5:15.

229 2 Cor. 5:16.

230 George R. Knight, *Anticipating the Advent: A Brief History of Seventh-day Adventists* (Boise, ID: Pacific Press, 1992), 112.

231 Liston Pope, *The Kingdom Beyond Caste* (New York: Friendship Press, 1957).

232 Haley Goranson Jacob, *Conformed to the Image of His Son: Reconsidering Paul's Theology of Glory in Romans* (Downers Grove, IL: IVP Academic, 2018), 3.

233 Rom. 8:29.

234 Rom. 8:28.

235 John 1:1.

236 Ronald Rolheiser, *The Holy Longing* (New York: Doubleday, 1999), 79.

237 Stanley Hauerwas and William H. Willimon, *Resident Aliens: A provocative Christian assessment of culture and ministry for people who know that something is wrong* (Abingdon Press: Nashville, 1989), 23.

238 Stanley J. Grenz, *Theology for the Community of God* (Grand Rapids: William B. Eerdmans Publishing Co. and Vancouver, British Columbia: Regent College Publishing 2000, 23).

239 Rom. 12:4-5.

240 Rowan Williams, *Christ: The Heart of Creation* (London: Bloomsbury Continuum, 2018), 55.

241 See books such as Jay David, ed., *Growing Up Black: From slave days to the present—25 African Americans reveal the trials and triumphs of their childhood* (Avon Books: New York, 1992); Debby Irving, *Waking Up White and Finding Myself in the Story of Race* (Cambridge, MA: Elephant Room Press, 2014); and Daniel Hill, *White Awake: An honest look at what it means to be white* (Downers Grove, IL: IVP Books, 2017).

242 Homer U. Ashby, Jr., *Our Home Over Jordan: A Black Pastoral Theology* (St. Louis: Chalice Press, 2003), 72.

243 Albert J. Raboteau, *Slave Religion: The 'Invisible Institution' in the Antebellum South* (New York: Oxford University Press, 1978), 123.

244 Fiorenza, "Paul and the Politics of Interpretation," 45.

245 Ibid., 45.

246 Delores S. Williams, *Sisters in the Wilderness: The Challenge of Womanist God-Talk* (Maryknoll, NY: Orbis Books, 2005), 2.

247 James H. Cone, *God of the Oppressed* (Maryknoll, NY: Orbis Books, 1997), 57.

248 David G. Benner, *The Gift of Being Yourself: The Sacred Call to Self-Discovery* (Downers Grove, IL: IVP Books, 2004), 30.

249 "Baptism," www.newworldencyclopedia.org/entry/Baptism.

250 John 19:15-19.

251 Luke 22:32.

252 Matt. 16:16.

253 Matt. 16:18.

254 1 Pet. 1:1.

255 Willimon, *Peculiar Speech*, 13.

256 James Baldwin, *The Amen Corner* (New York: Vintage Books, 1998, reprint), 9.

257 Thurman, *The Creative Encounter*, 40.

258 Gal. 3:28.

259 Raymond E. Brown, *An Introduction to the New Testament* (New York: Doubleday, 1996), 126.

260 Rev. 1:7.

261 Walter Brueggemann, *A Way Other Than Our Own: Devotions for Lent* (Louisville, KY: John Knox Press, 2017), 2-3.

262 T.B. Maston, *The Bible and Race* (Nashville: Broadman Press, 1959), 26.

263 Thurman, *The Inward Journey*, 40.

264 Willie James Jennings, *After Whiteness: An Education in Belonging*, (Grand Rapids: William B. Eerdmans Publishing Co., 2020), 11.

265 Pope, *The Kingdom Beyond Caste*, 21.

266 Thomas Gossett, Race: *The History of an Idea in America* (Oxford: Oxford University Press, 1997), 36, 37.

267 Ps. 62:11.

268 Eugene Peterson, *Subversive Spirituality* (Grand Rapids: William B. Eerdmans Publishing Co., 1997), 4-5.

269 Isa. 40.3.

270 Mal. 3.1.

271 Cf. Luke 1:41-44.

272 Cf. 2 Kgs. 1:8, 9:11-13.

273 Peterson, *Subversive Spirituality*, 5.

274 Debra J. Dickerson, *The End of Blackness: Returning the Souls of Black Folk to Their Rightful Owners* (New York: Anchor Books, 2004), 3.

275 Acts 10:47.

276 Acts 15:8-9.

277 Lucille Clifton, *Mercy* (Rochester: BOA Editions, Ltd., 2004), 59.

278 bell hooks, *Skin Again* (New York: Disney, 2004).

279 Eph. 4:5.

280 John 17:21-23.

281 W.E.B. DuBois, *Dusk of Dawn: An Essay Toward an Autobiography of a Race Concept* (1940, repr., Piscataway, NJ: Transaction Publishers, 2005), 59.

282 Rom. 12:2.

283 George D. Kelsey, *Racism and the Christian Understanding of Man* (New York: Charles Scribner's Sons, 1965), 25.

284 Andrew Root, *Faith Formation in a Secular Age: Responding to the Church's Obsession with Youthfulness* (Grand RapidsI: Baker Academic, 2017), 7.

285 The Studio Museum in Harlem's 2001 exhibition "Freestyle" is an example of post-black art; the term has been linked to *The End of Blackness* by Debra Dickerson, while others argue it was coined by Thelma Golden and Glenn Ligon at the Freestyle show.

286 See books to include: Efrem Smith, *The Post-Black & Post-White Church: Becoming the Beloved Community in a Multi-Ethnic World*; Kenneth A. Mathews and M. Sydney Park's *The Post-Racial Church: A Biblical Framework for Multiethnic Reconciliation.*

287 Juliana Menasce Horowitz, Kim Parker, Anna Brown, and Kiana Cox, "Amid National Reckoning, Americans Divided on Whether Increased Focus on Race Will Lead to Major Policy Change," Pew Research Center, https://www.pewresearch.org/social-trends/2020/10/06/amid-national-reckoning-americans-divided-on-whether-increased-focus-on-race-will-lead-to-major-policy-change/, Oct. 6, 2020.

288 Matt. 3:17.

289 Walter Brueggemann, William C. Placher, and Brian K. Blount, *Struggling with Scripture* (Louisville, KY: Westminster John Knox Press, 2002), 12.

290 Alice Walker, *We Are the Ones We Have Been Waiting For: Inner Light in a Time of Darkness* (New York: The New Press, 2006).

291 Eph. 6:5, Col. 3:22.

292 Dorothy E. Smith, *The Conceptual Practices of Power: A Feminist Sociology of Knowledge* (Boston: Northeastern University Press, 1990). Dorothy E. Smith (1996) "The relations of ruling: a feminist inquiry," Studies in Cultures, Organizations and Societies, 2:2, 171-190, DOI: 10.1080/10245289608523475.

293 J.K. Riches, *Galatians Through the Centuries*, Blackwell Bible Commentaries (Malden, MA: Blackwell Publishing, 2008), 209.

294 N.T. Wright, *Paul: A Biography* (New York: Harper One, 2018), 2.

295 Matt. 25:40.

296 Phil. 3:5-6.

297 Acts 17:28.

298 Toni Morrison, ed. *James Baldwin: Collected Essays* (New York: The Library of America, 1998), 784.

299 Ibid., 5.

300 Thomas Ryan, "Toward a Positive Spirituality of Body," in *Reclaiming the Body in Christian Spirituality*, Thomas Ryan, ed. (New York: Paulist Press, 2004), 23.

301 Jim Marion, *Putting on the Mind of Christ: The Inner Work of Christian Spirituality* (Charlottesville, VA: Hampton Roads Publishing Co., Inc., 2000), 198.

302 Cornel West, *Prophesy Deliverance! An Afro-American Revolutionary Christianity* (Anniversary Edition) (Louisville, KY: Westminster John Knox Press, 2002).

303 Thomas Merton, *The New Man* (New York: Farrar, Straus, and Giroux, 1961), 64.

304 While likely a myth, the creation narrative in Gen. 3:8-11 offers a lens through which to understand the human being's relationship to/with God and present miscommunications.

305 Thurman, *The Creative Encounter*, 152.

306 William Francis Allen, Charles Pickard Ware, and Lucy McKim Garrison, comps., *Slave Songs in the United States* (Bedford, MA: Applewood Books, 1867), 28.

307 Cyril, *St. Cyril of Jerusalem's Lectures*, 61.

308 Frantz Fanon, *Black Skin, White Masks* (New York: Grove Press, 1967), 11.

309 Dwight N. Hopkins, *Down, Up, and Over: Slave Religion and Black Theology* (Minneapolis: Fortress Press, 2000), 39.

310 Ibid., 27

311 Joseph Barndt, *Becoming an Anti-Racist Church: Journeying Toward Wholeness* (Minneapolis: Fortress Press, 2011), 59.

312 Sidney W. Mintz and Richard Price, *The Birth of African-American Culture: An Anthropological Perspective* (Boston: Beacon Press, 1992), 5.

313 Fanon, *Black Skin, White Masks*, 10.

314 Robert Jensen, *The Heart of Whiteness: Confronting Race, Racism, and White Privilege* (San Francisco: City Lights Publishers, 2005).

315 Brian Bantum, *Redeeming Mulatto: A Theology of Race and Christian Hybridity* (Waco, TX: Baylor University Press, 2010), 19.

316 Emily Bernard, *Black Is the Body: Stories from My Grandmother's Time, My Mother's Time, and Mine* (New York: Vintage Books, 2019).

317 David Brion Davis, *The Problem of Slavery in Western Culture* (Oxford: Oxford University Press, 1966), 447.

318 Karenga, Speech at Pomona College, Feb. 16, 1967.

319 The struggle to choose between cultural, racialized identity and Christian identity has also been explored in books to include Kimberly Cash Tate's *More Christian than African-American... and other ways Jesus turned my life upside down* and *What Does It Mean to be Black and Christian? Pulpit, Pew, and Academy in Dialogue, vol. 2: The Survival of a Whole People: The Meaning of the African-American Church*, ed. Forrest E. Harris Sr.

320 Fanon, *Black Skin, White Masks*, 30.

321 Eugene Peterson, *A Long Obedience in the Same Direction: Discipleship in an Instant Society*, 2nd ed. (Downers Grove, IL: IVP Books, 2000), 25.

322 Brueggemann, *A Way Other Than Our Own*, 18.

323 Thurman, *Luminous Darkness*, 105.

SELECTED RACELESS BIBLIOGRAPHY*

*When anti-racism isn't enough and being an ally doesn't clarify whose side you're on in the fight for justice

Achebe, Chinua. *Things Fall Apart*. New York: Anchor Books, 1994.

Alexander, Michelle. *The New Jim Crow: Mass Incarceration in the Age of Colorblindness*. New York: The New Press, 2012.

Allen, James Allen, ed. *Without Sanctuary: Lynching Photography in America*. Los Angeles: Twin Palms Publishers, 2000.

Anderson, Carol. *White Rage: The Unspoken Truth of Our Racial Divide*. New York: Bloomsbury, 2016.

Antum, Brian. *The Death of Race: Building a New Christianity in a Racial World*. Minneapolis: Fortress Press, 2016.

_____*Redeeming Mulatto: A Theology of Race and Christian Hybridity*. Waco, TX: Baylor University Press, 2010.

Blackman, Douglas A. *Slavery by Another Name: The Re-Enslavement of Black Americans from the Civil War to World War II*. New York: Anchor Books, 2008.

Blum, Edward J. and Paul Harvey. *The Color of Christ: The Son of God and the Saga of Race in America*. Chapel Hill: The University of North Carolina Press, 2012.

Bordewich, Fergus M. *Bound for Canaan: The Epic Story of the Underground Railroad: America's First Civil Rights Movement*. New York: Amistad, 2005.

Campbell, Bebe Moore. *Your Blues Ain't Like Mine*. New York: Ballantine Books, 1992.

Carter, J. Kameron. *Race: A Theological Account*. Oxford: Oxford University Press, 2008.

Chafe, William A., Raymond Gavins, and Robert Korstad with Paul Ortiz, Paul Parrish, Jennifer Ritterhouse, Keisha Roberts, and Nicole Waligora-Davis. *Remembering Jim Crow: African Americans Tell About Life in the Segregated South*. New York: The New Press, 2001.

Chestnutt, Charles W. *Conjure Tales and Stories of the Color Line*. New York: Penguin Books, 1992.

Christie, Ron. *Acting White: The Curious History of a Racial Slur*. New York: St. Martin's Press, 2010.

Cone, James. *The Cross and the Lynching Tree*. Maryknoll, NY: Orbis Books, 2011.

_____*God of the Oppressed*. Maryknoll, NY: Orbis Books, 2006, 9th printing.

_____*A Black Theology of Liberation: Twentieth Anniversary Edition*. Maryknoll, NY: Orbis Books, 2002.

_____*God of the Oppressed*. Maryknoll, NY: Orbis Books, 2006, 9th printing.

_____*For My People: Black Theology and the Black Church*. Maryknoll, NY: Orbis Books, 2002, 12th printing.

Douglas, Kelly Brown. *The Black Christ*. Maryknoll, NY: Orbis Books, 2002.

Dray, Philip. *At the Hands of Persons Unknown: The Lynching of Black America*. New York: The Modern Library, 2003.

DuBois, W.E.B. *The Souls of Black Folk*. New York: Penguin Books, 1989.

Ellison, Ralph. *Invisible Man*. New York: Modern Library, 1980.

Felder, Cain Hope. *Race, Racism, and the Biblical Narratives*. Minneapolis: Fortress Press, 2002.

_____*Troubling Biblical Waters: Race, Class, and Family*. Maryknoll, NY: Orbis Books, 1993, 10th printing.

Gerbner, Katharine. *Christian Slavery: Conversion and Race in the Protestant Atlantic World*. Philadelphia: University of Pennsylvania Press, 2018.

Gossett, Thomas F. *Race: The History of an Idea in America*. New York: Oxford University Press, 1997.

Gumbs, Alexis Pauline. *Undrowned: Black Feminist Lessons from Mammals*. Edinburgh, Scotland: AK Press, 2020.

Hahn, Steven. *A Nation Under Our Feet: Black Political Struggles in the Rural South from Slavery to the Great Migration*. Cambridge, MA: The Belknap of Harvard University Press, 2003.

Haney, Ian Haney. *White by Law: The Legal Construction of Race*. New York: New York University Press, 2006.

Hannah-Jones, Nikole. *The 1619 Project: A New Origin Story*. New York: One World, 2021.

Hart, Drew G.I. *Trouble I've Seen: Changing the Way the Church Views Racism*. Harrisonburg, VA: Herald Press, 2016.

Harvey, Paul. *Through the Storm, Through the Night: A History of African American Christianity*. Lanham, MD: Rowman & Littlefield Publishers, Inc., 2011.

Haynes, Stephen R. *The Last Segregated Hour: The Memphis Kneel-Ins and the Campaign for Southern Church Desegregation*. Oxford: Oxford University Press, 2012.

hooks, bell. *Black Looks: race and representation*. Boston: South End Press, 1992.

_____*Yearning: race, gender, and cultural politics*. Boston: South End Press, 1990

Hurston, Zora Neale. *How It Feels to Be Colored Me*. Carlisle, MA: Applewood Books, 2015.

Ignatiev, Noel. *How the Irish Became White*. New York: Routledge, 1995.

Jennings, Willie James. *After Whiteness: An Education in Belonging*. Grand Rapids: William B. Eerdmans Publishing Co., 2020.

_____*The Christian Imagination: Theology and the Origins of Race*. New Haven, CT: Yale University Press, 2010.

Jensen, Robert. *The Heart of Whiteness: Confronting Race, Racism, and White Privilege*. San Francisco: City Lights Publishers, 2005.

Johnson, James Weldon. *The Autobiography of the Ex-Colored Man*. New York: Dover Publications, Inc., 1995.

Jones, Robert P. *White Too Long: The Legacy of White Supremacy in American Christianity*. New York: Simon & Schuster, 2020.

Jones, William R. *Is God a White Racist? A Preamble to Black Theology*. Boston: Beacon Press, 1998, reprint.

Katznelson, Ira. *When Affirmative Action Was White: An Untold History of Racial Inequality in Twentieth-Century America*. New York: W.W. Norton & Co., 2005.

Larsen, Nella. *Passing*. New York: Penguin Books, 1997.

Lawton, Georgina. *Raceless: In Search of Family, Identity, and the Truth about Where I Belong*. New York: Harper Perennial, 2021.

Leong, David P. *Race & Place: How Urban Geography Shapes the Journey to Reconciliation*. Downers Grove, IL: IVP Books, 2017.

Litwack, Leon F. *Trouble in Mind: Black Southerners in the Age of Jim Crow*. New York: Vintage Books, 1999.

Haney, Ian Haney. *White by Law: The Legal Construction of Race*. New York: New York University Press, 2006.

Lorde, Audre. *The Master's Tools Will Never Dismantle the Master's House*. United Kingdom: Penguin Books, 2017.

Lowry, Beverly. *Harriet Tubman: Imagining a Life*. New York: Anchor Books, 2007.

Lum, Kathryn Gin. *Heathen: Religion and Race in American History*. Cambridge, MA: Harvard University Press, 2022.

Magee, Rhonda V. *The Inner Work of Racial Justice: Healing Ourselves and Transforming Our Communities Through Mindfulness*. New York: TarcherPerigree, 2021.

Makem, Resmaa. *My Grandmother's Hands: Racialized Trauma and the Pathway to Mending Our Hearts and Bodies*. Las Vegas: Central Recovery Press, 2017.

Mead, Margaret and James Baldwin. *A Rap on Race*. Philadelphia: J.B. Lippincott Co., 1971.

Mills. Charles W. *The Racial Contract*. Ithaca, NY: Cornel University Press, 1997.

Mintz, Sidney W. and Richard Price. *The Birth of African American Culture: An Anthropological Perspective*. Boston: Beacon Press, 1992.

Morrison, Toni. *The Origin of Others*. Cambridge, MA: Harvard University Press, 2017.

_____*Paradise*. New York: Plume, 1999.

_____*The Bluest Eye*. New York: Plume, 1994.

_____*Playing in the Dark: Whiteness and the Literary Imagination*. New York: Vintage Books, 1992.

_____*Sula*. New York: Plume, 1982.

_____*Tar Baby*. New York: Plume, 1981.

Morrison, Toni, ed. *Baldwin: Early Novels & Stories*. New York: Literary Classics of the United States, Inc., 1998.

_____*Baldwin: Collected Essays*. New York: Literary Classics of the United States, Inc., 1998.

_____*Baldwin: Collected Essays & Memoirs*. New York: Literary Classics of the United States, Inc., 1998.

Murray, Albert. *The Omni-Americans: Black Experience & American Culture*. New York: De Capo Press, 1990.

Omi, Michael and Howard Winant. *Racial Formation in the United States: Third Edition*. New York: Routledge, 2015.

Painter, Nell Irvin. *The History of White People*. New York: W.W. Norton & Co., 2010.

Patterson, Orlando. *Slavery and Social Death: A Comparative Study*. Cambridge, MA: Harvard University Press, 2018, reprint.

Patterson, Stephen J. *The Forgotten Creed: Christianity's Original Struggle Against Bigotry, Slavery, & Sexism*. New York: Oxford University Press, 2018.

Perkinson, James W. *White Theology: Outing White Supremacy in Modernity*. New York: Palgrave McMillan, 2004.

Powery, Luke A. *Becoming Human: The Holy Spirit and the Rhetoric of Race*. Louisville, KY: Westminster John Knox Press, 2022.

Raboteau, Albert J. *Canaan Land: A Religious History of African Americans*. Oxford: Oxford University Press, 2001.

_____*Slave Religion: The 'Invisible Institution' in the Antebellum South*. New York: Oxford University Press, 1978.

Roediger, David R. *How Race Survived U.S. History: From Settlement and Slavery to the Obama Phenomenon*. New York: Verso, 2008.

_____*The Wages of Whiteness: Race and the Making of the American Working Class*. New York: Verso, 2007.

_____*Working Toward Whiteness: How America's Immigrants Became White: The Strange Journey from Ellis Island to the Suburbs*. New York: Basic Books, 2005.

_____*Colored White: Transcending the Racial Past*. Berkeley: University of California Press, 2002.

_____*Towards an Abolition of Whiteness: Essays on Race, Politics, and Working-Class History.* New York: Verso, 2000, reprint.

_____*The Wages of Whiteness: Race and the Making of the American Working Class.* New York: Verso, 1991.

Roediger, David R., ed. *Black on White: Black Writers on What It Means to Be White.* New York: Schocken Books, 1998.

Rothstein, Richard. *The Color of Law: A Forgotten History of How Our American Government Segregated America.* New York: Liveright Publishing Corp., 2017.

Russell, Kathy, Midge Wilson, and Ronald Hall. *The Color Complex: The Politics of Skin Color Among African Americans.* New York: Anchor Books, 1992.

Smedley, Audrey and Brian D. Smedley. *Race in North America: Origin and Evolution of a Worldview*, 4th ed. Boulder, CO: Westview Press, 2012.

Smith, Clint. *How the Word Is Passed: A Reckoning with the History of Slavery Across America.* New York: Little, Brown, and Co., 2021.

Sollors, Werner. *Interracialism: Black-White Intermarriage in American History, Literature, and Law.* Oxford: Oxford University Press, 2000.

Sowell, Thomas. *Race and Culture: A World View.* New York: Baker Books, 1994.

Sterling, Dorothy, ed. *The Trouble They've Seen: The Story of Reconstruction in the Words of African Americans.* New York: De Capo Press, 1994.

Thurman, Howard. *Deep River: The Negro Spiritual Speaks of Life and Death.* Richmond, IN: Friends United Press, 1990, reprint.

_____*The Luminous Darkness: A Personal Interpretation of the Anatomy of Segregation and the Ground of Hope.* Richmond, IN: Friends United Press, 1989, reprint.

_____*The Search for Common Ground.* Richmond, IN: Friends United Press, 1986.

_____*Jesus and the Disinherited.* Boston: Beacon Press, 1976.

_____*The Creative Encounter.* Richmond, IN: Friends United Press, 1972, reprint.

_____*Disciplines of the Spirit.* Richmond, IN: Friends United Press, 1963.

_____*The Inward Journey.* Richmond, IN: Friends United Press, 1961.

Terkel, Studs. Race: How Blacks & Whites Think & Feel About the American Obsession. New York: The New Press, 1992.

Tisby, Jemar. *The Color of Compromise: The Truth About the American Church's Complicity in Racism.* Grand Rapids: Zondervan, 2019.

Terkel, Studs. *Race: How Blacks & Whites Think & Feel About the American Obsession.* New York: The New Press, 1992.

Villarosa, Linda. *Under the Skin: The Hidden Toll of Racism on American Lives and on the Health of Our Nation.* New York: Doubleday, 2022.

Wilder, Craig Steven. *Ebony & Ivy: Race, Slavery, and the Troubled History of America's Universities.* New York: Bloomsbury Press, 2013.

Wilderson, Isabel. *Caste: The Origins of Our Discontents.* New York: Random House, 2020.

Willimon, William H. *Peculiar Speech: Preaching to the Baptized.* Grand Rapids: William B. Eerdmans Publishing Co., 1992.

_____*Who Lynched Willie Earle? Preaching to Confront Racism.* Nashville: Abingdon Press, 2017.

Wise, Tim. *Colorblind: The Rise of Post-Racial Politics and the Retreat from Racial Equity.* San Francisco: City Light Books/Open Media Series, 2010.

Rowe, Sheila Wise. *Healing Racial Trauma: The Road to Resilience.* Downers Grove, IL: IVP Press, 2020.

Wright, Richard. *Native Son.* New York: Perennial Classics, 1998.

_____*Uncle Tom's Children.* New York: Perennial Classics, 1991.

Zizioulas, Jean. *Being as Communion: Studies in Personhood and the Church.* Crestwood, NY: St. Vladimir's Seminary Press, 1985.

Printed in the USA
CPSIA information can be obtained
at www.ICGtesting.com
JSHW011755071123
51411JS00004B/17